THE HEART OF AFRICA

A STORY OF A MISSIONARY KID GROWING UP IN BURUNDI, AFRICA

MARILYN KELLUM BARR

WESTBOW PRESS
A DIVISION OF THOMAS NELSON
& ZONDERVAN

Copyright © 2023 Marilyn Kellum Barr.

All rights reserved. No part of this book may be used or reproduced by any means, graphic, electronic, or mechanical, including photocopying, recording, taping or by any information storage retrieval system without the written permission of the author except in the case of brief quotations embodied in critical articles and reviews.

WestBow Press books may be ordered through booksellers or by contacting:

WestBow Press
A Division of Thomas Nelson & Zondervan
1663 Liberty Drive
Bloomington, IN 47403
www.westbowpress.com
844-714-3454

Because of the dynamic nature of the Internet, any web addresses or links contained in this book may have changed since publication and may no longer be valid. The views expressed in this work are solely those of the author and do not necessarily reflect the views of the publisher, and the publisher hereby disclaims any responsibility for them.

Any people depicted in stock imagery provided by Getty Images are models, and such images are being used for illustrative purposes only. Certain stock imagery © Getty Images.

New American Standard Bible®, Copyright © 1960, 1971, 1977, 1995, 2020 by The Lockman Foundation. All rights reserved.

ISBN: 978-1-6642-9027-3 (sc)
ISBN: 978-1-6642-9028-0 (hc)
ISBN: 978-1-6642-9026-6 (e)

Library of Congress Control Number: 2023901218

Print information available on the last page.

WestBow Press rev. date: 02/01/2023

DEDICATIONS

In loving memory of my mother and father Esther Perry Kellum and Robert Dean Kellum.

In loving memory of my uncle Everett Kellum and my cousin David Kellum.

Special thanks to Mae Kellum, Lorna Kellum Long, Neil Kellum, Zana Kellum, and Paul Kellum for assistance in providing reports of more recent events and pictures.

Special thanks to my husband Thomas Edward Barr for his technical support and content advice.

CONTENTS

Chapter 1   The Heart of Africa 1
Chapter 2   Early Preparation for Burundi 5
Chapter 3   A Long Trip, Fun for Us but Hard Work for Dad 9
Chapter 4   Shopping in a New Country 15
Chapter 5   Urugos 23
Chapter 6   Schools 29
Chapter 7   Cape Tomato Cobbler 35
Chapter 8   Chameleons 41
Chapter 9   Playtime 45
Chapter 10 Roads and Paths 47
Chapter 11 Saturdays 51
Chapter 12 Jiggers (Not Chiggers) 55
Chapter 13 Chance Meetings, or Were They? 59
Chapter 14 Rain, Many Helpers, and a Car 61
Chapter 15 Giving Thanks and Building a Station 67
Chapter 16 Nkundwa 73
Chapter 17 Monkeys and Bananas 77
Chapter 18 Going on Safari 85
Chapter 19 Rift Valley Academy 89
Chapter 20 A Hike in Rift Valley 93
Chapter 21 Other Plans 97
Chapter 22 As the Years Go By 103

Suggested Places to Contribute 111
Sources 113

CHAPTER ONE

THE HEART OF AFRICA

When we use the word *heart,* we might mean several different things. Initially, we might mean the physical beating heart in a living thing. This might suggest the source of life as the heartbeat is a sign of life and energy. It also connotes something necessary to meaningful existence. Burundi, when seen on a map, clearly is shaped like a human heart, and it is the centermost country in Africa, somewhat like the location of a heart in the center of the chest. The tiny country is nestled below Rwanda, east of Congo, west of Kenya and Tanzania, and southeast of Uganda. As a colony of Belgium, along with Rwanda and the Democratic Republic of Congo, Burundi became independent in 1962, shortly before we arrived. Burundi is where I spent my life from age thirteen to sixteen. Living in boarding schools most of the time, I had to look within myself for strength and the ability to center on my purpose for life. My travels and experiences gave me a valuable education beyond any school.

Another meaning of the word *heart* is a source of emotion. The use of *heart* in songs and poems usually represents love or other strong emotions. One might say someone had a *heartache* when the object of love is missing. Or someone sends *heartfelt greetings,* meaning strong feelings of concern and well-wishing. I learned to care about the people of Burundi and loved my experiences that held so many positive influences on me in this beautiful place. I can say that I left part of my heart in Burundi, or I kept many memories in my heart when I had to leave. Most of the people of this country lived in poverty, but there was priceless beauty in the landscape and some of the most pleasant weather all year anyone could imagine. We were located just below the equator, yet mountain altitudes gave us cool temperatures. In addition, we had an entirely different view of the stars, seeing the southern cross as the prime constellation rather than Orion of the Northern Hemisphere. What a new view of the planet earth we saw!

A third meaning of the word *heart* is referring to the soul or spiritual center. The heart of man may exude good or evil, depending on the choices one makes that will either build hope and faith or corrupt the inner self. I saw in the common people of Burundi a contentment in their meager lifestyle that defies understanding at times. Some of the world's poorest people might have wished for more possessions, but they held no resentment for their neighbors who had more. What I saw was their desire for peace, which they called *amahoro*. They included this word in their greeting, "Bgake nedza, amahoro," which wishes peace for everyone they met. In Kirundi, the *b* sound is a unique combination of *b* and *v*, whereby one does not fully close the lips while humming the sound. The *r* sound is also softer, like the rolled *r* of French and Spanish.

I was glad to live a simpler life than one I might have had in America. These years overseas were a happy time that did give me a peace that this was the perfect place for me to spend these formative teen years of my life. Burundians did not always have peace as there were constant struggles for government power among those hoping for positions in government, but they continued to wish for it for themselves and all those who were dear to them.

To understand Burundi's people, one must know the population consisted of three tribes or ethnic groups. The Tutsis, also called Watutsis, were historically royalty; they were taller and had more narrow noses and faces and were known for being animal tenders. The Hutus were, by far, the majority of the population; they were average in height, and most of them lived as farmers. A tiny group, known as the Twa, were Pygmies; they lived in small villages hidden in the jungle, where they hunted and gathered their food as they wandered from place to place. Kirundi ("Kee-roon-dee") is the native language, while French is the legal language since the Belgian colonization. Burundi ("Bvoo-roon-dee") and Rwanda ("Goo-anda") are twin countries that have the same languages and tribes, although they each have separate governments. In 1962, Belgium gave independence to these countries, along with the Democratic Republic of Congo. Belgian colonists, who had built many schools, businesses, towns, and roads, abandoned the countries, but their influence was used to appoint the king, known to be a Tutsi prince. There were coups and uprisings between the two main tribes, but they shared government power and later held elections.

My family moved to Burundi (Urundi) in 1963, planning to get government approval to start a Christian radio station. My parents Bob and Esther, my two brothers Neil and Paul, and I arrived in Bujumbura (Usumbura) in February of that year. After six months of meetings, documents, and letters between many native Christians, other missionaries, and my father, government officials approved Radio Cordac, or CABCO, along with a school to train several Burundian men in radio work. We stayed for four amazing years filled with powerful learning experiences in culture, faith, and accomplishment.

Previously, other members of our family had lived and worked in Central Africa. We were greeted by our cousins, David and Mae Kellum, who were working there. David ran an automobile repair business and a training school for local men to learn the trade. He also helped build churches and a bridge across a treacherous river and repaired a wide variety of things used by the missionaries. They would help us get acquainted with the people and places, and we lived in their house for a time, while they were gone back to America for furlough.

In the previous generation of the Kellum family, my uncle Everett was superintendent over as many as three hundred schools in Kenya, which had previously been colonized by England and later given its independence. My aunt Ruth was a nurse. They raised two children, one of whom was David, who served in Burundi.

CHAPTER TWO

EARLY PREPARATION FOR BURUNDI

When my parents met in high school, they soon became close friends. My mother graduated as valedictorian in a class of four, and my father graduated the same year. They had made their own class yearbook by hand, so they were developing communication and publishing skills back then. My mother started college majoring in math and home economics, a good traditional career for a woman, until she and my father decided to get married. At that point, she joined in my father's vision to spread the Gospel in a new way, radio. Finding Azusa Pacific College, they learned Christian leadership, along with a full range of technical and communication skills particularly geared toward work in Christian radio stations around the world. In the previous generation, my mother's grandmother had a career ahead of her time, opening a fig preserves factory in her hometown. There were preachers and missionaries in my mother's and father's heritage. My parents would learn the science and technology of radio operation. Both learned Morse code and ham radio in the days when huge tubes and metal boxes were part of the equipment. Dad would brag about my mom passing the ham radio test and getting her certification first. Seeing the big picture was my dad's gift, while my mom's expertise was in the details.

After their graduation from the college in California, my dad took a job as a preacher in a church in Orange County. Two years after I was born, my parents joined the Far East Broadcasting Company, which sent them to the Philippines. In telling their story years later at family gatherings, my parents joked about me and moaned about my mother as we crossed the Pacific Ocean on a freighter ship. We faced our first experience with typhoon-scale storms as my mother, pregnant with my brother Neil, suffered so much nausea, she nearly died of dehydration. The rest of the crew and my dad were sick too, but I was the frolicking two-year-old, untouched by the storm or seasickness.

With all of us surviving the torrential storm, my brother was soon born in the Philippines, and my parents began their new jobs that put their training to good use. There was an existing station in Manila, where we lived for four years, the typical term for missionaries overseas. Dad's job was mainly geared toward keeping the equipment operational and planning needed upgrades. Mom's job was focused on editing tapes for various recorded programs. Mom could work at home while she took care of me and my new brother Neil, who was now a citizen of two countries, the Philippines and the good old USA. I do not remember much of this time, but we have some great pictures of the four of us in our traditional Filipino garb of starched, heavily embroidered linen men's shirts and winged-sleeved dresses. I was told years later that I had been bitten by a rabid little dog that came out from underneath our house elevated on blocks to help against the frequent flooding of that humid island. Thankfully, I forgot getting the shots in my stomach.

When we went back to South Texas, we lived in a small house owned by our church, and Dad began preaching at different churches around the country and meeting people who were interested in supporting the mission work. Our next assignment was to go to Japan for six months in the winter. My second brother Paul was born before we left. Our house had paper walls and cold cement floors where Mom tried to keep my baby brother warm to little avail. I had been sick so frequently that Mom gave up and taught me at home. I don't know if I told anyone, but the teacher would hit our fingers with a ruler whenever she didn't like something we did. My parents believed in giving spankings when we deserved them, but I tried hard not to ever need one; however, I never knew what I had done at school. I was scared just watching her hit someone else. I wonder how much that contributed to my illness, but I suspect the weather and my fear contributed to it. On a brighter note, I did enjoy learning some Japanese. When Mom and Dad bought me a kimono, parasol, and elevated wooden shoes, I would sing a hymn in Japanese I repeated many times in churches back in America. The song was "Rolled away, rolled away, rolled away, every burden of my heart rolled away" or, in Japanese, "Uki nu, uki nu, uki nu, cocorona omoniwa, uki nu."

Our time in Japan was cut short to six months as we were transferred to Okinawa for the next three-and-a-half years. Each of the three countries had Christian radio stations that served the local island as well as beaming to long-range destinations where Christian missionaries were barred from teaching the Gospel. The towers beamed a signal where programs in other languages could reach distant places to encourage Christians as well as to teach new followers of Christ in lands that did not have religious freedom.

We moved to Okinawa after our stay in Japan. My parents' jobs were similar to what they had done in the Philippines. The weather seemed perfect most of the time, but there were a couple of typhoons where corrugated metal roof material was wrapped around electric wire in the high winds. Mostly, though, I felt very safe riding the public bus to my little school for missionary kids and to a pool on a nearby military base with my neighborhood friend. I had learned to swim first in the ocean, where we would curl our legs up and flap our arms to not have to step on the spiny sea urchins. Our house had the best backyard in the neighborhood, and all the other kids would come enjoy the huge sandpile, swings, and little swimming pool. We never picked the places we lived in, but that place was my favorite.

One tragedy occurred shortly before we left Okinawa as a fire broke out at the Quonset hut housing the radio studio facilities, destroying everything. My father worked hard to rebuild what he could in the time we had before we left. After completing our term, it was back to South Texas, only a few months later, we moved back to California, believing we would go back to some Far East Pacific island, but this was not to be. Instead, it became clear to my parents God had something else planned for them, so back to Texas we went, and my dad attended numerous meetings with interested sponsors and churches in America. My mother's notes included the special message of God, "Commit your way unto the Lord; trust also in Him; and he will direct your paths" (Ps. 37:5). As they searched for confirmation this was God's plan for them, she recorded the verses: "Then you will discern the fear of the Lord, and discover the knowledge of God. For the Lord gives wisdom; from His mouth comes knowledge and understanding" (Prov. 2: 5–6). It was a new project, but it still followed the principle of Jesus's directive to His disciples when He said, "Go therefore and make disciples of all the nations, baptizing them in the name of the Father and the Son and the Holy Spirit, teaching them to observe all that I commanded you; and lo, I am with you always, even to the end of the age" (Matt. 28:19–20).

CHAPTER THREE

A LONG TRIP, FUN FOR US BUT HARD WORK FOR DAD

Our trip to Burundi included many stops, some of necessity and others because we did not want to miss out on seeing some important places along the way. Mom and Dad always said traveling was a special kind of education, and we agreed. My mother's diary gives the following account of our business stops in America:

> Tuesday, February 5, 1963 – We left Houston International Airport for Wichita, Kansas at 6:30 p.m. Friends and relatives from Friendswood and Paul's Union, La Marque, were there to see us off.
>
> Wednesday, Feb. 6 – Rested today and made-up packing lists for shipment.
>
> Thursday, Feb. 7 – Met at the second Executive Committee of the Central Africa Broadcasting Co. Bob given title of Advance Director for Africa and arrangements made to send out letters to raise further needed funds and details worked out for our going. In the evening we celebrated Marilyn's birthday with a dinner and then a birthday cake and gifts afterwards. Grandpa was also present.

> Friday, Feb. 8 – Got CABCO stationery and envelopes printed, calling cards, and school books for children ordered. Said goodbye to Leon Brown and Papa – then left Wichita with James Morris for Cleveland, Ohio via Chicago. That night it was very cold in Cleveland, about 0 degrees, with snow on the ground. We were put up in the house of the Teague's who were on vacation in Florida. Ethel (a single lady who lived with them) made our stay very enjoyable.

The Teague's were members of the church where Dad would present the Christian radio project at the Sunday evening church service. These meetings and presentations were an integral part of organizing and gaining support for carrying out the plan in Burundi. We continued our journey as Mom reports:

> Monday, Feb. 11 – We left early in the morning for Washington D. C. with James Morris. We went by taxi to the Continental Hotel where we stayed that night. Bob and James had appointments in the afternoon.
>
> Tuesday, Feb. 12 – We took a tour of Washington D. C. by taxi while Bob and James had business appointments. We saw the U.S. Mint (saw bills printed, trimmed, cut up, sorted, and counted), the White House, drove by the Lincoln's Memorial, Jefferson Memorial, Washington Monument, Smithsonian Institute, Archives Building and the Capital Building. This tour lasted almost 4 hours. We came back to the Hotel, packed our bags, ate lunch, and went on another short tour of the Arlington Cemetery, the changing of the guard at the tomb of the Unknown Soldier, and Robert E. Lee's home. While there we fell in with a tour conducted for two small girls – one of them was Caroline Kennedy we were told when we were leaving. We went on to the airport where

we waited for our flight to New York where we arrived late at night.

Wednesday, Feb. 13 – We did not take the morning flight to London as planned because we waited to see if we could get our Burundi visa that day. We went after breakfast on the bus and subway (freezing weather) to uptown New York to see RCA – Radio City New York. We took a tour, ate lunch, then waited while Bob contacted Associated Press office and called the airline. Our visa was not yet available. I was suffering from dizzy spells, but we decided to go on our way to London that night. We left for the airport at 6:00 p.m. and took the 8:00 p.m. flight to London. So, it was goodbye U.S.A. for now.

Thursday, Feb. 14 – Having lost five hours during the six-hour flight to London, we arrived at about 7:50 a.m. We were checked in with no problems. We took an airline bus to a temporary terminal, where we got a taxi to take us to St. Ermins Hotel where we had reservations. We waited while our rooms were prepared, ate breakfast, and then went to bed, as we were very tired. We slept until about 5:00 p.m. We ate a snack in the evening, played games, and went to bed.

Friday, Feb. 15 – We had breakfast, rested, and played games while Bob had a business appointment. We then packed and moved to the Foreign Mission Guest House at noon. We had lunch and made reservations to leave London on Monday for Geneva, hoping to pick up our visa in Athens before our flight to Usumbura the 25th.

Saturday, Feb. 16 – We left early for downtown London for a sightseeing tour given by Thames Tours. We went on a bus with the guide calling out the various districts and points of interest. The highlight of the tour was our visit to the Houses of Parliament, Westminster Abbey, and the changing of the guard. We got cold while watching the latter but it was all very interesting. We ate lunch in a little restaurant where we had European food.

Sunday, Feb. 16 – We were allowed to sleep a little late on Sunday morning. Breakfast was at 9:00 a.m. and soon afterward we left by bus for Westminster Chapel. We got off at Green Park, walked through the park and past Buckingham Palace to the Chapel. Rev. Lloyd-Jones spoke on "How we may know that we are Sons of God." The hymns were sung from words only. The service lasted from 11:00 a.m. until 12:30 p.m., so we rushed back to the bus and arrived home just in time for dinner. After dinner we took off again. The Reverend and his wife, child, and her parents welcomed us with an English tea. Many pastries, cakes, and sandwiches were served. We had a fine visit with them, and they expressed interest in the C.A.B.C.O. project. We came home by surface train and subway, and then bus. It took almost two hours each way.

As you can see, our travels included some sightseeing, but for my father, most of his time was spent making contacts with other Christians who might help support the radio station. Along the way, we experienced British customs and food in a private home, an experience not necessarily available to tourists. It is also clear we found the need to have the proper paperwork permitting us to live in Burundi, even if it required extra stops on our trip.

Monday, Feb. 17 – We stayed at the Foreign Mission House while Bob went into downtown London to the Belgium Embassy to see if they could issue Burundi visas. They could not, and we finally learned that the only Burundi Consul was in Brussels, and only they could issue Burundi visas. So, our schedule to go to Brussels was made for that evening on Sabena at 8:00 p.m. At noon he had a luncheon engagement with F. Livingston Hogg at his factory that services U.S. professional test equipment. His manager director David Rennie is chairman of a new radio organization formed to assist missionary radio around the world. Upon his return to the Guest House, we prepared to leave for the airport by taxi and the plane trip to Brussels. We arrived in Brussels in one hour and moved into the Queen Anne Hotel.

Tuesday, Feb. 18 – We rested late in the morning. Bob called the airline and began working on our visas again. Then he contacted some local missionaries – the Winstons who knew the Wheelers and others and had some former contact. We also met a representative of HCIB who travels in Europe seeking to build radio stations. He came over in the evening and talked with Bob about others interested in radio in Africa. We ate at a self-service or cafeteria type place. The food here is good with lots of French bread, good meat, etc. We found out we could not make the Wednesday flight to Usumbura, so we decided to stay in Brussels until the Saturday flight.

Saturday, Feb. 23 – Started packing to go to the airport by 11:00 a.m. We took a taxi to the Sabena Terminal downtown and checked in our baggage there. We then rode a train to the airport. We boarded the DC-7 plane and flew for three hours to Rome where we had an hour to walk around the terminal. We then boarded the plane again for our last flight to Usumbura. They served lunch and supper on the plane. We settled down as best we could for the long night on the plane.

Sunday, Feb. 24 – We were awakened early – about 5:00 a.m. by the plane captain to get ready to eat our breakfast and prepare to land in Usumbura. It was light, and we could see the jungles far below us. We ate, washed up, and about 6:30 a.m. sighted Usumbura and Lake Tanganyika. We circled twice to set down. We could see some white faces to meet the plane. Mae and David Kellum were there and another missionary, Gerald Bates. We were also met by an American Consulate official. We had no trouble because we had the right visa – one from the Burundi Consulate in Brussels. They had us open only two suitcases. We were in Burundi, and after loading our baggage, we went to the Mission Guest House at Vugizo on a hill overlooking the city and lake. We rested and the children went to English Sunday School. That evening we ate supper at the Bill Johnson home."

CHAPTER FOUR

SHOPPING IN A NEW COUNTRY

We arrived in Bujumbura, which is the name I will call it; my mother called it Usumbura, which was its earlier name. We had traveled from the northeast of America and Europe at the coldest part of the winter to a country just south of the equator, where it was their summer. We were hit by a blast of hot air. Our feet had felt stiff as we walked in the freezing temperatures, and now we could feel our feet swelling from the heat. We were eager to change into lighter clothes and cooler shoes. We had a few things, but most of our clothes were for the trip. Our summer clothes were coming later by ship in barrels, along with our house items. We would have to pick up our shipment in Dar es Salaam on the coast of Tanzania.

> Monday, Feb. 25 – We spent most of the day in Usumbura going to various shops with David and Mae Kellum and Paul and Leona Thornburg. I bought a pair of Italian sandals and we bought two interesting carvings of gazelles. Tomatoes and bananas were plentiful, but stores selling American or European goods were small and poorly stocked. The Africans spoke French, Kirundi, and Swahili. Some Greek merchants spoke English. At noon we ate a picnic lunch on the shore of Lake Tanganyika. The children wanted to wade in the water, but we were warned it carried a terrible disease caused by snails …

Disappointed with not being able to swim, we went back into some shops. My brothers Neil and Paul and I liked the clear jelly plastic sandals in bright colors. These sandals had been poured in a mold in one piece. We each got a pair. They were cheap and comfortable enough. Shops in the city were mostly run by people from India or Europe. People who moved here from other countries would have their furniture shipped from abroad or carved locally with hand tools. Burundi did not have factories or industry. Almost all natives were farmers. Only in cities were there a few other options.

When we needed to buy groceries, there were no stores like we were used to at all, where one store sold every food we wanted. Instead, African men would bring baskets of vegetables and other wares to sell to the missionaries at our homes or in open areas like flea markets. If we wanted bread or something baked, we would go into a locked pantry, where we could find imperishable foods like sugar, flour, shortening, cake mixes, and gelatin packages. Missionaries were dependent on churches in America to send barrels with these food items. This was our store of another kind, but it sufficed. The weevils liked the flour too, so we always had to sift it before we used it. We hired an African man who had been trained to bake bread and a wide variety of other things. Mom would set up a menu with him, and she would prepare something for us on his day off. There were rare butcher shops to buy meat in cities. Mom's variety of responsibilities kept her busy full time outside of the home. She taught my brother Paul first grade, since our boarding school started with second grade. She typed documents, letters, and flyers and worked with the other missionary ladies to teach sewing and Bible lessons.

When we kids grew, we were needing bigger clothes, which we sometimes got as hand-me-downs from other missionary families. Also, my mother sewed dresses for herself and me. We would have to go to the city to find a fabric shop. The farmers of Burundi did not cut up and sew their material like we did. They would buy several yards of bright bold-patterned prints of cotton fabric and wind it around their bodies and over one shoulder. The men and women dressed similarly, except the women chose bolder colors. Babies might only wear an oversized shirt without any diaper. Boys might sometimes have a shirt and shorts, but girls dressed like their mothers in a wrap of fabric. Women wore their hair short and did not wear head wraps. Women and girls always dressed modestly in skirts, wraps, or dresses that covered their knees, never in pants. Missionary women and girls followed this custom as well. Africans who were more educated and were employed by the government, businesses, or missionaries would wear more modern shirts, pants, and skirts, which were available in shops in the city. Foreigners from India, China, and European countries owned the shops and imported the clothes or fabrics from their countries. Before fabrics were imported, Africans made bark cloth by beating fibers from palm trees. It was dark and scratchy.

For me, when I needed a dress, I looked through the two-inch-thick catalog we had brought with us. We called it "the wish book." I wished I could order a dress for myself, but I just looked for ideas of what I might like. Then I asked my mom if she could teach me how to sew. Unfortunately, she did not have the time, so I did the best I could on my own. We found fabric and a pattern in a shop in the city, and I began to pin and cut out the pieces like I had watched my mother do before. Mom showed me how to operate the sewing machine, and I put the pieces together and hand-sewed the hem. This dress was the only one I would take when I went to high school later besides my two uniforms.

If we were interested in souvenirs, some Africans were skilled at carving, painting, or making musical instruments, woven baskets, and beaded miniature weapons. They carved beautiful gazelles and ebony elephants, which they offered to sell to us. They managed to use hand-forged knives, sandpaper, and oils for polish. They made miniature drums of gazelle skin and a round hollow wooden piece with open ends on both sides. They would weave strips of the skin to pull the top and bottom pieces of leather together over the ends. To tap the beat, the drummer would use his bare hand or a stick. Another sound instrument was a thumb piano, or kalimba, made of a small wooden box with a hole in the center and small pebbles inside, which one could shake for added percussion. The keys for playing a tune were narrow pieces of metal that were held down to the sound box with wire. The metal pieces were different lengths to make different notes like a piano. One could hold the instrument in both hands while plucking the metal pieces with both thumbs. Another amazing artistic skill the Africans developed was the embellishment of miniature weapons with colorful small beads in geometric designs. While we were in Burundi, we managed to collect some of these beautiful curiosities. The Africans made their own pots and baskets as well, mostly for their own use, but they made some with decorations and designs that would attract foreign shoppers as well. Africans were very gifted in artistic endeavors and music.

The only grocery store I ever saw in Africa was in Nairobi, Kenya, where we stopped to buy snacks on our way to the high school I attended for ninth and tenth grade. We were so excited to be able to buy chips, cookies, and candy that we would save as long as we could at our dorm.

The open-air market is where the average people of Burundi would make their purchases, sales, or exchanges. Congregating at a set time in an open area in many places all over the country, the people would manage to barter for foods or find some of the foreign salesmen who had wares for sale, such as cloth or factory-made items, such as radios or bicycles. Men would come to our houses with baskets of vegetables from their gardens. Manufactured products were primarily made in foreign countries like India or China. The poor farmers of this land would have to exchange perhaps a portion of their crop to get what they wanted for a larger purchase. Tools each family needed were machetes and hoes, which could be purchased or hand-made. The growing of coffee and tea in the hills were the prime cash crops, which the native people were paid to tend and harvest, but foreign businessmen were involved in sales and shipping. The average income of Burundi's farm people was about the lowest in the world, but advanced education or skills gave some of them the chance to rise above the poverty level of most.

As missionaries, our families lived here without many things taken for granted in America, but we adapted to a simpler life, appreciating the happiness we witnessed in these people who had far less than we did. Sometimes our parents would explain to us kids we would have to cut down on our spending because donations from America were lower than usual. We did not have air conditioning or television, but we never went hungry or without plumbing and electricity like so many of the poor. Sometimes we felt ridiculously wealthy in some of the places we stayed and in viewing some of the most beautiful scenes or important sites around the world as we traveled. We felt blessed to do without some of the things we were used to having in America because we could learn to be less dependent on material things to be happy.

Our family, like other missionary families, adopted the attitude of this verse: "Not that I speak from want, for I have learned to be content in whatever circumstances I am" (Phil. 4:11).

Kalimba, or thumb piano

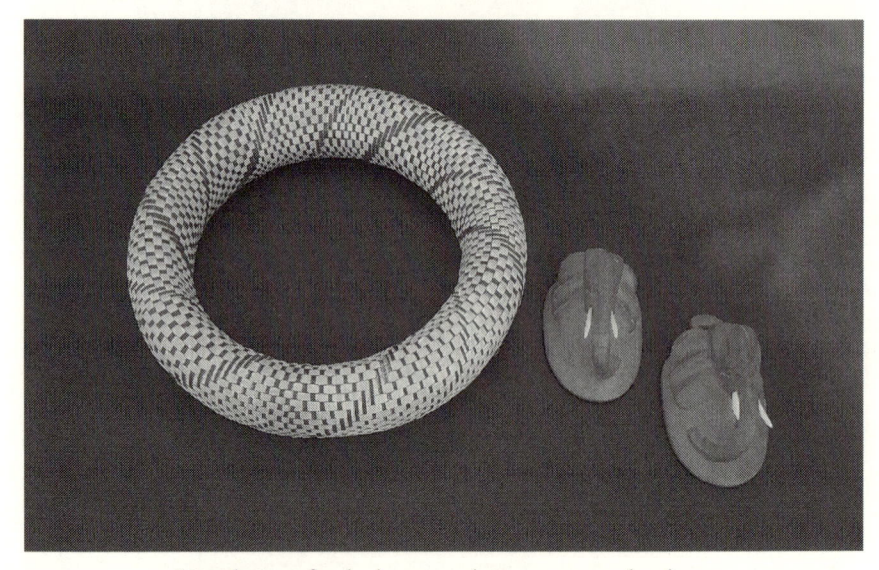

Head ring for balancing large pots or baskets
and elephant heads with ivory tusks

Small ebony elephants

Bujumbura with Lake Tanganyika and Congo it the background

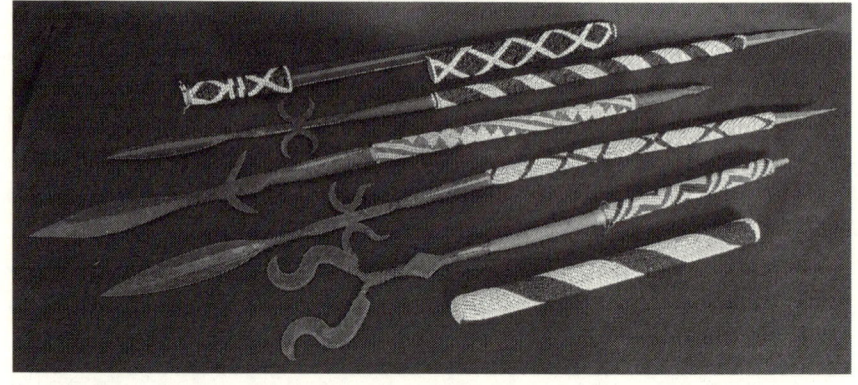

Miniature sheathed knife, spears, grass cutter, and club are decorated with seed beads in blue or red with white seed beads

CHAPTER FIVE

URUGOS

Bright green banana trees surrounded the small dwelling of the rural, peace-loving Africans of this country. Their simple circle-shaped homes were about twelve feet in diameter. By packing mud between two boards, they made their own sun-dried bricks used for the walls. Dry grass was mixed into the mud to hold the bricks together. Once the bricks were dried, stacked, and joined by the same red mud, more mud could be smoothed on both sides of the wall like stucco. Sometimes the walls were made of poles stuck into the ground with tall grass filling in the open spaces. Rough tree poles could then be positioned on the top as a support for a roof made of tall grass. One small door opening allowed the family to enter and exit, the taller people bending over for the short doorway. The walls were not much above five feet high, except in the middle, since standing inside was unusual. These huts had no windows or doors, since they were not considered a necessity, and glass-framed windows and wooden doors were not affordable or practical. The dwelling was mainly for sleeping. No beds or other furniture softened the family's rest. Bare dirt, dry grass, or leaves were the only mattresses in these dwellings. Each person may have had their own blanket.

Outside the dwelling, the family would do their cooking on an open fire and congregate part of the daytime. The man of the house would spend his day watching the cow or goat and guiding them with a long staff to other grassy areas to feed. On market day, he might take some vegetables to sell. Otherwise, he would relax outside the home with his banana beer and maybe a battery-operated radio.

To enclose the small open area of the *urugos*, these poor farmers grew a holly green hedge of stiff, spiny stems. Serving as a fence, it kept out snakes and other unwelcome wildlife while keeping their precious cattle, goats, and chickens in for the night. If animals or people tried to push through these hedges, the stems would poke their skin, or if the stems were broken, a poisonous milky liquid would seep out that would deliver a painful irritation. The hedge did not have to be very high to serve as an effective barrier around the dwelling.

The young children, wearing only an oversized shirt or wrap, would toddle around the open area inside the hedge. When the mothers or big sisters went out to work, babies were tied to their backs with a long piece of cloth wound around the baby's bottom and tied around the waist of the person carrying the child, while the upper edges were tied around the upper chest or shoulders of the mother or sister. I don't remember seeing a child crawling around freely or playing with any toys. Mostly babies spent their days with their arms and legs dangling out of the cloth and their heads turned to the side to breathe. Older boys would run around in a shirt and shorts or a wrap around their waist. Mothers or sisters would go about their chores of hoeing in the fields or carrying water pots on their heads, while the baby rode on their backs. They could carry quite a heavy load by using a doughnut-shaped woven ring sitting on the crown of their heads. I admired how straight their posture was and how gracefully they could walk carrying so much weight. Crop tending, food preparation, water collection, and childcare were designated as women's chores, while the men and boys spent much of their time tending to the cattle and taking produce to market for sale. Those who might own a bicycle could take their produce for sale in the cities. It was amazing to see what huge loads they could balance and tie to their bicycles.

Beyond the hedge were banana trees and other taller trees, creating a jungle, although there were no vines to swing on like in the movies. Few wild animals hid in the thick growth, except monkeys and snakes. Burundi was too heavily populated for large animals like elephants or wildebeests. No large open prairie existed in this part of Africa for herds of animals or predator beasts. This area of Africa was mostly hillsides with *urugos*, or dwelling areas, separated by some trees or small open fields. A family farm plot was smaller than a basketball field. Good grassland was thinned down by the growing population. Fishing was good in the rivers and in the valley, where Lake Tanganyika lay and the Democratic Republic of Congo's thick forests could be seen on the other side of the lake. Hippos enjoyed the cool lake water, and people knew to leave them alone.

The steeper mountainsides, however, were scored with beautiful terracing of dark fertile land. The primary cash crop grown on these terraces was some of the richest coffee in the world. We were told it was exported to Europe and the United States. Previously, Belgium had colonized Congo, Burundi, and Rwanda. In Burundi, Belgians encouraged the use of the rich land on the mountainsides for growing coffee and tea. In addition, the altitude provided cooler temperatures. It was hard to believe daytime temperatures were mild and nights were actually quite cool, even though the country was located just below the equator. Burundians would maintain and harvest the coffee and tea, while foreign businessmen would arrange shipping abroad.

Usually, the foods Burundian people prepared were mashed, starchy plantain-type bananas, beans, maize, peas, and eggs. Some families might have a single long-horned cow that might provide milk for the children, if they were blessed to own one. Beef was not a staple of these people, but they might sell the meat to foreigners in the country or to butcher's shops in the towns. A bony goat or a few chickens might also be kept in the open area of the *urugo*. The goat and chickens were only eaten at special feasts.

I never saw children with toys besides sticks or abandoned bicycle wheels. Boys would roll these bike wheels down the road by holding a stick in the tireless groove and pushing it in an upward motion. They would take turns, running down the path or road together until they got their turn. The boys would also help their fathers care for the animals. There were no villages with chiefs. This lifestyle reminded me more of the individual farms where America's first pioneers would build sod homes, only there were no horses, plows, buggies, wells, or towns to buy things nearby. Land spaces for the Africans, however, were much smaller. Each family might have a hoe and a machete to do all their farming. Most manufactured goods were too expensive or unavailable to these poor farmers in Burundi. To people in the cities or on missionary compounds, houses were built of cement and corrugated metal. Likewise, only these houses had electricity or plumbing.

These simple farmers seemed content with their way of life. All they seemed to hope for was a chance to raise their children in peace. They were friendly to missionaries and glad we could help them with medicine and education. Some missionaries would teach the farmers how to fertilize their fields. Missionary women held classes where African women would learn how to cut out shirts or quilt blocks and hand-sew them together. They would have a devotional while they were together as well.

Women carrying hand-woven baskets

Two urugos and adjacent fields of crops

Family assembles to listen to radio while mother
crushes cassava roods for bread

CHAPTER SIX

SCHOOLS

To get to our boarding school, we had to drive about four hours up the steep hills from Bujumbura to Mweya, nicknamed Windy Hill, a community with homes for three missionary families, our dorm building, our schoolhouse, and a Bible school to train African preachers. Three missionary family homes had been provided by a particular denomination's missionary organization, and each family received their salary and various supplies from their church's donations. All three missionary families were there to train Burundi's men, who had completed primary school, to become preachers for their own people. For four years, they were taught the Bible, speaking skills, and languages needed for translation by missionaries and African leaders. The students could speak and write in Kirundi, the primary native language; French, the language of the Belgian colonists; and English, the language of the American missionaries. When we arrived in the community, we drove past the preachers' school and the missionaries' houses to get to our dorm house, which held about twenty missionary kids whose parents served as missionaries in Burundi. The kids were in second through eighth grade. Our dorm parents had two rooms in the dorm as well.

Occasionally, parents could pick up their kids for the weekend, but each school term lasted three months, when all of us would go home for a month. This was much more practical for allowing young kids to go home three separate months spread out more often for those parents who could not come so easily during a term. In between visits to our parents' homes, our dorm held one big family, it seemed. Besides a hallway of bedrooms on each side of the dining hall and dorm parents' rooms, we had a large gathering room for meetings and worship services. There was one full bathroom with a tub across from the dorm parents' rooms and a tiny half bathroom in the girls' wing. The kitchen was on the far side of the dining hall.

Our dorm parents, Ralph and Esther Choate, were near retirement age, but they had volunteered to stay and take care of the school for missionary kids for a few years. They had worked with the African people for many years, starting Christian schools, churches, and a medical clinic. When we arrived, they supervised us, while Ralph taught at the Bible school. The woman's first name was the same as my mother's, and I soon became fond of spending time talking to her and teasing her, like when I tied about fifteen extra knots in her apron strings in back. She had spent most of her life in Burundi from childhood and knew the Kirundi language fluently. Our dorm father was in a wheelchair, but he still went out to do mission work. Our dorm mother did most of the supervision of meals, tending a garden, getting us to bed, and getting us off to our school building in the morning. She also went out to do translating of sermons and other mission work. Sometimes she translated for my dad's sermons at African services.

All the buildings were up on a hill, where a nice breeze blew much of the time, hence the name Windy Hill. The altitude was high enough that we had no need for fans to cool off the inside. In the evenings, we called it "sweater weather." I never remember sweating there, unless I was running or digging in the dirt as we often did on our free time. We definitely needed our blankets at night.

By walking about a football field's length in short weeds, we could be in our school building. It was built out of bricks in a plain rectangle with a one-gabled roof. Entering the door in the center of the front wall, we were in an open area with three student desks. There were two other rooms, one on either side of this center area, which could be classrooms, but only the one on the right was being used. We only had one teacher for grades 2–8. We each had our own desk, and the teacher had her own desk with a blackboard behind it. There were bookshelves for textbooks and a collection of other books, mostly classics for young readers, which served as our library for individual reading. This room might seem like a typical classroom, but there was a long bench next to one side of the teacher's desk. This was the proverbial one-room schoolhouse. Less traditionally, the teacher did not address the entire classroom for teaching. Students in each grade would be called up to the bench, where we received our lesson and papers. The teacher would show math problems on the blackboard behind her or write key instructions or information for us. Then the students in that grade would go back to their desks to complete their lesson in that subject. All the students stayed busy with various lessons given that day or the day before. If we finished everything we had been given to do, we could pick a book from the bookshelves or continue reading a book we already had. Another technique our teacher used was peer-teaching, especially with math for older kids. Those in our grade would meet out in the open room to share our answers for each problem and discuss our figures and steps until we had all settled on which answer was correct and why. At first, this seemed like cheating, but it actually ended up being a good method for learning from one another. There were two other students in my grade, and we worked well together.

Our teacher was very adept at multitasking and organizing activities to keep everyone busy and learning. She guided us to keep us focused on the correct things, but she let us be in charge of our own learning. We felt satisfied with ourselves when we gathered on the bench to show what we had accomplished and got our next directions. She could encourage us with kind words and instructions in a brief amount of time. I don't honestly remember any students making disruptions or playing around in this teacher's classroom. I decided in the sixth grade that I either wanted to be an English or a math teacher when I grew up. I took books back to our dorm and read them at night under the covers with my flashlight after we had been tucked in for the night. We had quite a few classic literature and history books I read this way.

My brother was in the fourth grade, and I was in the sixth when we started at Mweya. Our parents came for short visits sometimes because there was a ham radio set up on this compound, where my parents went to talk to my grandpa and another relative who were helping organize the mission work and spread information to supporting churches. My grandpa had a tiny room for his ham radio on the third floor of the house. Sometimes Mom and Dad would take us home for the weekend. My little brother, Paul, was in the first grade, so he stayed at home. Mom helped him until he was in the second grade and could start going to Mweya. One weekend, when my parents and little brother came, my mom washed clothes at a missionary house and hung them outside. Some of the other kids from our school took my little brother's underwear off the line as a practical joke to embarrass us. It did.

The African children of Burundi were required to go to primary school for six years. Secondary school was only available for those few who could afford to pay. Their schools were taught in Kirundi and French. With a primary education, most of them returned to agricultural work and raising families. With a secondary education, some could train for jobs in the cities or some levels of nursing or technical skills. Universities in other countries could prepare a few students for careers as doctors, lawyers, and political leaders. Students who graduated from the preacher's school began to serve as preachers, moving to the area they would serve and receiving support from local people and American or European churches. One man, Nkundwa, who graduated from this school, became our interpreter, particularly for my father, to preach to local churches and to converse with government officials about the Christian radio station project while attempting to gain approval.

Ralph and Esther Choate, our dorm parents

Mweya dorm kids (I am back row center)

CHAPTER SEVEN

CAPE TOMATO COBBLER

Our boarding house dining room held two long tables with chairs for twenty or more kids to sit and eat all their meals. This big room in the center of the building was located between a hallway to the girls' bedrooms on one side and a longer open hallway on the opposite side with more bedrooms for the boys. Down the boys' hallway was a gathering room for church services and meetings. On the far wall was a piano used for services and for piano lessons and practice for some of the kids. I took lessons once a week and practiced occasionally, although I was not as enthusiastic about practice as I should have been.

Some of my key memories are associated with the dining hall. It was in that room we heard the announcement that Pres. John F. Kennedy had been assassinated. Also, we had our certificates attached to a ribbon with our name above it that displayed emblems representing passages we had memorized like Psalms 23, John 1, Corinthians 13, and the words of some well-known hymns. To this day, I frequently recall the words of these key passages and songs I would hold in my mind and heart for the rest of my life.

Eating in the dining room included some formal customs handed down by our dorm parents from generations of British rules. It seems odd I learned to value setting the table properly with the knife and spoon on the right and the knife blade facing in when we knew the African people ate with their hands or drank from a pottery bowl. The fork would go to the left of the plate, and if needed, a second smaller fork for salads was placed next to the regular fork. We had our plates filled by the African cooks hired to prepare all our meals. We sat down in our assigned places to begin eating. We could go back for more sometimes, but the strictest rule was we had to finish everything on our plate before we could get up and leave to go play.

We never went hungry, and most of the food was quite tasty and recognizable as foods Americans were used to eating. We had meat, but beef always came as ground hamburger. This was not because the cooks lacked a varied menu, but because no amount of cooking could make the African cow meat become tender. These cows were fed on open grassland, led around to greener areas by the farmers, but the cows were always underfed and probably old. Men would tap these bony cows on their backs with their long staff to move them to a greener area. The African cows were thin, as they were often on dry, dusty ground, where most of the grass had been eaten down. I was amazed to see the livestock's horns were longer and bigger than the longhorns Texas cattle were famous for. The African cow hides were solid rusty reddish brown, the same color as the dry dirt they stood on. When a cow was butchered, all the meat was ground up and frozen. Goats and chickens were only butchered and eaten by the Africans on rare occasions, and the eggs or milk were used or sold in the meantime. We had chicken for our meals at times, but we were never served goat meat in our dorm.

We had plenty of vegetables, such as green beans, broccoli, beets, carrots, and so on. There was a garden on the property, where some of these were grown, but we also obtained some vegetables brought to the house by African men carrying their produce on a three- or four-foot-wide flat basket, more like a tray, they would carry on their heads. They would bring the basket down to the ground where the dorm mother or cooks could choose what they needed to buy from them for our meals. Some of these vegetables were grown just for the missionaries who were used to these foods.

The Africans had a much more limited diet of cooked plantain bananas that were very starchy, and that I would compare to mashed potatoes. Corn and peas might be included, but protein sources were rare, except for beans. Some families had a cow or goat that gave them milk for the children.

One time our family visited a church for the weekend, where the Africans served us their best food, better than they usually ate. The special dish of the meal was goat innards, which, to them, was like Thanksgiving turkey, but seemed almost inedible to us. As a kid, I tried my best to eat everything on my plate, like I had been taught at school, never to waste anything. I failed to keep the rule that evening, although I did a better job eating the cooked bananas with goat gravy on top. I felt guilty I had wasted some of this delicacy served to us at such sacrifice.

Even as a kid, I understood food was scarce. In Burundi, as we traveled around in our van or took walks, we would see skinny kids and babies with the swollen bellies, not due to good nutrition, but of hunger and lack of proper food and milk. Still today, I picture in my mind the crying babies that were not getting the food they needed.

Fortunately, one of our boarding house activities was useful to add more vegetables to our available food variety and to teach us the responsibilities of growing our own food. Each of the kids had a rectangle of ground about ten feet by six feet, with boards marking the perimeter of our own garden plot. This was our own garden patch to dig, plant seeds, grow plants, and water whatever we picked. I had several different kinds of plants, but the most memorable one I had was a huge beet I let grow to a gigantic eight-inch diameter. When I finally decided to pull up my beet, I brought it into the house and took it to the kitchen to boil for my supper. We were allowed to prepare and eat our tiny farm produce all by ourselves, but I shared my beet with several others. I was very proud of my huge beet. Normally, most farmers harvest their plants before they get so large that they are tough and fibrous like mine. We had to chew a little harder, but the monster beet was tasty.

My boarding house mother had one vegetable she confessed she did not like. This, she said, was turnips. One time at supper, she carried around a small pan with boiled turnips. She told us she was offering them for us to try, but she said if we did not like them, we did not have to finish them. We were amazed by her humility and honesty since she had modeled perfect manners at all times. Many of us accepted a small helping of the turnips. I took some and did not find them distasteful at all. I ate all my helping and wondered why our role model found this veggie so inedible. At least she did not force us to eat something she didn't like. I appreciated and admired her understanding.

Breakfast was always hot cereal, except on Sunday, when we had homemade cinnamon rolls. They had a wonderful white icing and plenty of gooey cinnamon inside. The drawback to this Sunday treat was we had to take our quinine pill to prevent malaria, which anyone could get from mosquito bites. The pill left a bitter aftertaste that unfortunately mixed with the sweetness of the cinnamon roll.

There was a unique food we were served from time to time that was actually the one I wish I could decline. That was not, unfortunately, the boarding house way. Who would believe I might like to skip dessert? In this case, that's exactly what I wanted to do. Served in a small bowl, this fruit cobbler looked like a treat. The fruit was something I had never heard of until I had come to this place. It grew on a bush just outside my dorm room. The fruit was maroon in color, somewhat darker than a normal tomato. Several hung from the branches of the densely leaved bush. This fruit was called a cape tomato. The size was like a roma tomato, but it was rounder and darker and a little purplish. The bush was more like a decorative shrub than a tomato vine. They say tomatoes are really a form of fruit, but there could be no argument cape tomatoes were a mildly flavored fruit, not at all related to tomatoes. The cape tomato fruit was mixed with sugar, covered with a batter, and baked. The cobbler topping was more like cake than crisp and was not very sweet. The real problems I had with this fruit was the pulp was filled with hard seeds as plentiful as in raspberries but larger, and the flavor lacked tartness and sweetness. I would take small, slow bites, and I knew I was going to be there for a long time before I could finish. I tried not to bite down on the seeds, but it was hard to swallow. How could a dessert be so abhorrent to me? As the other kids got up and left their empty bowls and ran outside to play, I would sit and stare out the window, taking awkward bites. I am not sure, but I imagine it would take me thirty minutes to empty my bowl, at which time I would have earned my freedom. Sometimes I would notice my brother having to stay in his seat after everyone else had finished, so I knew there was a certain food that was hard for him to eat as well.

Later I would wonder whether I could have confessed to my dorm mother I had one food I could call inedible, like turnips to my dorm mother. Unfortunately, I never had the courage to discuss this with her and get permission to skip this dessert. Perhaps it was my stubbornness to not let this rule get me down. Gladly, I never saw cape tomatoes anywhere else in the world. Give me turnips any day, but not those cape tomatoes! At least my endurance through this minor hardship made me tougher, for I would face much greater challenges in the future.

It was not always easy to follow this verse, but we were certainly blessed with good food and pleasant company: "Always giving thanks for all things in the name of our Lord Jesus Christ to God, even the Father" (Eph. 5:20).

Our dorm house with my giant beet in the foreground

CHAPTER EIGHT

CHAMELEONS

Africa is well known for its exotic animals, especially lions, giraffes, various gazelles, zebras, ostriches, elephants, hippopotamuses, and rhinoceroses. These animals are rarely, if ever, tamed. Few large animals lived in Burundi because the human population was more plentiful, and some animals, like elephants, had been poached for their ivory. Uganda and Tanzania had game reserves, where elephants were protected and could be found. Africans did not have pets like dogs and cats because they were not available, and the average family were unable to feed them if they were available. If feeding themselves and their children was so difficult, they certainly lacked food for more than their goat, chickens, and cow, which would become food some day or provide eggs and milk in the meantime. Each family grew its own food, and if they lacked enough food for themselves, which often was the case, they went hungry. They certainly did not entertain the concept of pets.

On the other hand, like other American kids will find curious animals and turn them into pets, I found a chameleon native to the area. We found chameleons on the outside of our windows or on the shrubs around our dorm. We might find them as we played outside, capturing them and carrying them around to show off to the other kids. When I caught one, I carried it around in my hand while I looked for flies for it to eat. If I found a fly, usually on the window, I would slowly raise my pet a couple of inches from the fly and watch its long pink tongue shoot out of its mouth, pulling the fly back and swallowing it quickly.

It was exciting to see that two-inch sticky tongue do its work so well to capture its dinner. Then it was on to find another fly and another amazing performance of a strange lizard.

These chameleons were bright green with dark gray geometric designs on their backs. Their tails would curl behind them, but if they were fully stretched out, they were nearly a foot long. Their mouths looked like they were frowning like a grumpy old man. Their eyes stuck out like half a ball with two big eyelids covering the eyeball and leaving only a slit to see through. The eyeball could turn in any direction: front, back, up, down. Each eye was on the side of its head and could move separately. These reptiles had the perfect combination of eyes and tongue to catch its prey.

I had heard this creature would change color to match what it was standing on, but that was not the case. The chameleons, however, would change to a bluish green sometimes or a reddish green at others. Our room window had a glass pane that opened to the inside and a screen on the outside. This area between the screen and the glass made a perfect cage to keep my pet in. When I came back from school, I would run back to my room to get it and search for flies to feed it.

And now I have a confession to make. Occasionally, we would play pranks on our dorm mates. So, my chameleon died one day. I was sad, but I had a mischievous thought to put it between the sheets of the bed of one of the other girls in the other room. I should have thought about it a little longer, but my impulses had already kicked in. You have probably heard of short-sheeting someone's bed at camp or dormitories. First, I removed the top cover and loosened the bottom half of the top sheet, pulling it up to the pillow, creating a pocket where the person's legs would be stuck halfway down the bed. Then I stuck the chameleon down inside the pocket. The girl found it that night, but I never guessed the level of her reaction until the next afternoon as I came back from school, when the dorm mother told me I was going to have to sit in a chair facing the wall for a couple of hours for what I had done. I hoped no one would see me sitting there in the hallway because I never had been in trouble before. I had plenty of time to think about my bad choices that day. Yes, I knew feeling a cold reptile touching your leg when you crawl into bed was a disgusting and shocking experience when you were planning to get cozy. I regretted my deed and let the chameleons find their own dinner in their natural home outside after that. I realized I did not have the knowledge of how to care for the rare lizard either.

CHAPTER NINE

PLAYTIME

I know it might seem rather unnecessary to mention what a bunch of kids might do in their free time in a place that had no television and few toys, but I feel our playtime activities provided several positive influences on our character. First, we mostly played as a team. Second, we liked to play in the dirt and plan huge projects, which we created, planned, and completed together.

One of our longest and most complex projects was to build a huge network of roads and cities for the little three-inch-long metal cars we all had. There was plenty of bare dirt, and we had plenty of free time, so we used our hands to scrape the dirt together into raised highways and buildings that made us prouder and prouder as our structure grew into quite a city. We spent far more time on the dirty, sweaty work of building than we did in driving our little cars around. Likewise, our positive nature could be seen in how we treated one another as equals, even though our ages were years apart.

Another project we developed was building our own fort. First, we found some tools to dig up the dirt because our ground space was not level. That was our first mistake. We had shovels, sticks, hoes, and pickaxes for hard spots. We had to work close together as our team attempted to create a flat floor area on the side of a hill. I sustained a small injury to my ankle one afternoon. The person who accidentally hit me with the ax turned out to be my own brother. I think we abandoned this project before we built the walls and roof, although we had planned to gather lots of long sticks for support and tall grass for the walls and roof.

Every Friday night, after dark, was time to play fox and rabbits. A huge tree on the far end of the yard was home base, where all the rabbits could be safe, if they were touching it. One of us would be the fox that could catch a rabbit by touching them and turn them into the fox. This was as close to any sport we had available at Mweya.

If we did play alone, we might play in our rooms or go out to ride bikes or strap skates onto our shoes and roll around in a small circle on the cement slab meant for parking. Looking back, I feel I didn't miss any fun kids growing up in America had. In a letter from my friend back in Texas, she mentioned there was a group of four men who had a very popular band. She said they were called the Beatles. I had never heard of them and didn't care.

CHAPTER TEN

ROADS AND PATHS

Burundi had a few rusty-red dirt roads constructed around the green hillsides of the country, slicing through the terraced patches of crops like a quilt in various shades of green. America had supplied a variety of those yellow land-moving machines to carve out the hills and level the roads. Only one of the roads going up the hills was ever paved, but it always needed repairs from areas that would wash out in the heavy rains. Someone had mentioned, occasionally, these useful machines meant to help develop a transportation system for this nation were "borrowed" by government officials to develop their own properties. These roads were all hardly wide enough for two-way traffic, so we would have to slow down and move carefully to the side to pass any car or truck coming toward us. Fortunately, there were huge trees on the descending side of the hill to keep cars or trucks from falling down the hill. This more developed road had a checkpoint, where anyone who used it was required to have the appropriate paperwork to be able to pass. The blacktop road was longer to get us to our various missions in the hills or down to the valley of Lake Tanganyika, where Bujumbura lay situated just across Congo. On the other hand, the other road was shorter in distance but was so rough that cars could hardly get through. Both roads had huge potholes and were subject to landslides and torrential rains. The roads going up through the mountains wound around the hillsides with steep cliffs on one side and steep downhill slopes on the other. The missionaries would often share transportation by riding together when required for business in the capital. Gitega was a smaller town, though quite important for government and business, but it did not have much paving either.

I remember the trips up and down the shorter dirt road, which was faster unless it had rained recently. The mud holes could become traps for our cars and delay us for hours. There were no gas stations or public buildings of any kind along the roads. No police frequented the roads for speeders or roadside assistance. There were no streetlights, stoplights, or speed limit signs. We were at the mercy of the mud. Nine months of the year, September through May, were called the rainy season. June through August were winter since we were south of the equator. These months were not much cooler, but they were drier. The lush green vegetation would turn yellow.

About once a month, my brother Neil and I would go home for the weekend from our school in Mweya. For the first few months, our family lived with other missionaries until a house was left empty by our cousins who returned to America. This was not a particularly long trip, but when Radio Cordac (French wording) or CABCO (Central Africa Broadcasting Company) was approved by the government officials, we had a much longer and more monotonous trip down to our apartment in Bujumbura. To entertain ourselves in the back seat of the car, we would sing, "The ants go marching one by one, hurrah, hurrah. The ants go marching one by one, hurrah, hurrah. The ants go marching one by one, the little one stopped to suck his thumb, and they all go marching down, to the ground, to get out of the rain, boom, boom, boom. The ants go marching two by two … the little one stopped to tie his shoe."

We sang verse after verse of this song, giggling in the back seat. Strangely, no one told us to stop. Singing our song and acting silly must have been God's way of protecting us from seeing some Africans' bodies along the side of the road. When we heard our parents talking later, the people must have been killed by the Tutsi militia, trained and armed men serving the government. Hutu men were taken from their homes at night and killed or taken to prisons. These activities were mostly kept hidden from the news, so we did not talk about them further. Most of the Hutu men taken or killed were the best educated Burundians, which included the native preachers.

Another example of the growth of transportation was the one airport in the country, in Bujumbura. Missionaries would enter the country or leave it from this location. There was one blacktop runway, a tower, and a small building with a customs counter, all guarded heavily by Burundi soldiers holding automatic rifles. No jets could land there because the runway was too short for them. It was here we would have to show our visas, passports, and contents of every bag. We would be required to fill out a form asking us what we were carrying, including exactly how much money we had with us. People could gather outside the building to watch the passengers coming in or going out, waving at one another from a distance. I had been nervous seeing the soldiers, but we did not feel threatened since we had all our paperwork, and we believed God would protect us as we were there to do his work.

Most of the Africans, however, did not use the roads or the airport for transportation. Most of them did not have cars or even bicycles. Their only form of transportation was the paths carved deep into the red dirt by the tread of many bare feet calloused by a lifetime of walking on rough terrain. There were often women with their babies tied to their backs and huge pots of water balanced on their heads or men with walking sticks and a cow or flat baskets on their heads, taking their vegetables to market.

On Saturday afternoons, while I was living at the school for missionary kids, we would take walks down these paths through the country. Our dormitory mother would take us on a variety of adventures over the hillsides around our school. I contemplated on how these paths were the roads of Burundi's native people, but they guided us to meet the native people and the places they went since long ago.

While we walked on these paths, the people we met were friendly, and our dorm mother spoke to them in fluent Kirundi. We kids would smile as we walked by them, and they would smile back at us. We had the opposite reaction when snakes crossed our path. Some snakes were quite poisonous, like black mambas, but even nonpoisonous pythons were large and could do some harm. We yelled as we scattered off the path and looked around to avoid any snake along the way. Also getting our attention were the nine-foot-tall white ant or termite hills that rose from an open field. Some people ate the termites fresh from the hill, and others would collect a batch of them to fry in oil. On another trip, we saw some pygmies silently appear from out of the thick vegetation. They were, in fact, as short as some of us kids. They were all men dressed in loincloths and carrying tall sticks. We stared at them in silence as they stared at us, realizing we were unusually privileged to see them. Perhaps they were as curious as we were about their lives and culture. These paths lead us to places few tourists would ever see. We never knew what or who we would see next.

Life gives us different roads or paths that we must choose wisely to remain near to God. The Word says, "Thou wilt make known to me the path of life; in Thy presence is fulness of joy; in Thy right hand there are pleasures forever" (Ps. 16:11). Our lives will include fearful moments and joyful moments, but we must choose to follow the path the Lord wants us to follow.

CHAPTER ELEVEN

SATURDAYS

My favorite day for the potential variety of activities was Saturday, but before the adventures began, we knew we had a schedule of duties. Saturday was bath day at the boarding house. With four inches of water in the only bathtub, we would take turns with girls from youngest to oldest and then boys in the same order in the same water. The two youngest girls would bathe together with their shared bar of soap and towel. We would wash our hair by dunking as best we could to wash and rinse without running any new water. When all the girls were finished, the boys took their turns by twos as well. We had saved water and felt satisfied we were clean enough until next Saturday. When I started to get older, I asked Aunt Esther if I could take my bath by myself, and she said my roommate and I could bathe alone.

After my bath, I curled my hair in pink sponge rollers I would leave in all day so I could have curly hair for Sunday. We would go on long walks to interesting places and see a variety of people who greeted us. We knew their Kirundi words "Bgake Nedza. Amahoro." This meant "Hello, Peace." Our dorm mother would say a few more words in Kirundi as we crossed paths, and they would converse with her for a little while. I wished we could understand more words in Kirundi.

One of the most memorable and significant trips we made was to the lesser-known source of the Nile. Livingstone and Stanley had searched for this wonder and found it and each other in Burundi. There was more than one place that had been given that name, but all locations were freshwater springs that bubbled up continuously. A cement basin was built around the area where the water came through the ground and out a faucet and then ran through a drain back down into the ground. We each had a chance to taste the cool, clear water. If our dorm mother had not known where to find this marvel, we certainly would have never known it existed. There were no roads or signs to guide tourists, and I believe it was a well-kept secret from almost everyone. The Nile that goes all the way up to the Mediterranean Sea through Egypt begins in the Rift Valley, which spreads across several countries in Central Africa. There are large lakes and rivers throughout this huge expanse of the continent, and somewhere farther south of each river might be a similar small spring. Lake Tanganyika to the west and Lake Victoria to the northeast were the two largest lakes in Africa, and both led to the giant life-giving river Nile. We were impressed with the significance of small things that can lead to much bigger natural wonders, and how vastly different cultures, like the Egyptians and sub-Saharan Africans, could be so uniquely linked on the same continent.

There I was with my pink sponge rollers in my hair, drinking from the source of the Nile with water on its way to the pyramids and the Mediterranean Sea.

Here at the source of the Nile, I, in my pink rollers, taste the pure spring water.

CHAPTER TWELVE

JIGGERS (NOT CHIGGERS)

When I was growing up in South Houston, my grandmother would warn me about going out in the garden behind her house. She had some okra growing, winding itself through some tall grass. She warned us there were chiggers out there. I had been attacked by those annoying tiny red chiggers that found a home in the layers of our skin. I had been bitten by the chiggers while just running around in the St. Augustine grass, and I feared those bugs on me that would not scratch off and itched for days. People would offer advice on how to get rid of chiggers by using alcohol, but the best method I remember was to put fingernail polish on them to suffocate them.

In Africa, I was about to meet a more annoying bug than I could ever have imagined. One weekend we were camping out with the Paul Thornburg family, who had three kids we went to school with. My dad was preaching for special services, and Mr. Thornburg was translating. Our family of five was staying in a Volkswagen bus converted into a camper with a sink, counter, cabinets, and a bench seat that converted into a bed. We also had a tent for additional sleeping space. On Saturday, we wandered around an open market, where the people had earlier been selling vegetables, eggs, and a variety of other things. My two brothers and I ran around with the other kids in the open areas, finding whatever adventures we could muster. The ground was bare and dusty since this spot was used frequently as an open market. We did not run around in any weeds because there was little but bare dirt in the area. Lurking in that dirt was a pest we would soon learn to fear.

On Sunday, we attended church services at the African church, a thatch awning resting on rough poles. Africans streamed in from all directions through the morning. They would seat themselves on roughhewn benches, waiting for more to arrive. There were no watches on their arms, and I imagined they didn't have calendars on the walls of their huts. I was amazed to see them gradually appear, walking as families or individuals beckoned by a bell ringing or drum beating well before service time. This was clearly the reason the service did not start at a precisely scheduled time.

Beneath the thatch roof, there were two rows of benches, one side for men and the other for women and children. This custom of separation was simply an African custom of propriety. Singing traditional hymns in the Kirundi language was a joyful experience that thrilled my soul. Everyone would sing loudly, almost shouting, without hymn books, led by a song leader, while another man kept a quick pace with a large deep-sounding drum. My dad preached in English and paused after every sentence to allow Paul Thornburg to translate into Kirundi. Services were several hours, but Africans were unaware of how long they had been there. There was always a call for special prayer for individuals who had come forward with spiritual needs. These Burundian people were very enthusiastic about their faith. They might be following the words of David when he wrote, "Break forth, shout joyfully together … For the Lord has comforted His people …" (Ps. 52:9).

As American children, we sat as quietly as we could, feeling the heat and the dry air around us. Our toes were beginning to itch, and we started scratching our toes in our dusty sandals, not knowing the cause. When the service was over, we returned to the VW bus. We hopped on the bed, whining to Mom to check out our toes. We had never felt such a localized itching, especially around our toenails. Mom tried to help us figure out what was going on, but she was as clueless as we were. The other family explained we had been attacked by jiggers. These tiny black wonders would burrow under the skin, laying eggs in little sacks around them. Mom found out she would have to dig them out with a needle, being careful not to break the egg sack. Poking into the oozing white bumps on our feet, we could clearly see the egg sacks that had to be removed. These egg sacks were about a quarter of an inch in diameter. First, Mom would have to open the skin above the egg sack and dig out the adult bug along with the babies. After this ordeal, our feet still itched for quite a while, so we would keep checking to see if we had gotten all those jiggers out.

As we later were told, these bugs mostly infested dry dirt, exactly like what we had been running around in all weekend. The three months known as the summer back in Texas, when the chiggers flourished in yards and gardens, were considered winter south of the equator. Located in a land that had no cold weather all year, winter was the dry season, which is when the jiggers flourished.

That weekend I learned to fear dry soil, not just because our feet were so dusty, but for those nasty jiggers hiding in it, waiting to nest in our toes. I still wonder how the Africans dealt with those jiggers, except I can imagine their bare feet were calloused so thickly that the jiggers didn't bother them. Those jiggers must have been excited to find us tender-footed Americans.

CHAPTER THIRTEEN

CHANCE MEETINGS, OR WERE THEY?

Friendly visits were often about meeting key people who could help those working to present the prospect of starting a Christian radio station become familiar with government officials before the process of paperwork began. Sometimes these meetings were planned, and sometimes they just seemed to happen randomly. Mom reported just such "random" meetings soon after we arrived:

> Monday, Feb. 25 – That evening Bob, David, and Paul went to the home of Mr. Gloie to tune his piano. He was the head of the U.S.I.A. Cultural Center.

> Tuesday, Feb. 26 – We finished our business in Usumbura in the morning. We were not able to complete our residence certificates because the Immigration Office was in the process of moving. We saw the U.S. Cultural Center, and Bob met Sindamuka, a Christian member of Parliament, at a filling station – just a chance meeting. After lunch we packed and left for Kibimba at 2:00 p.m. The drive up the mountain was beautiful with a sheer drop of over 1,000 feet. We arrived about 8:00 p.m. Dr. Rawson met us, welcomed us to the Randall Brown home for supper, doctored the boys'

sunburn, and gave us lodging in his house for the night. Mr. Lacey, head of the Alliance Radio Program, was at the station, so Bob talked to Randall concerning the possible radio project – It so happened?

After extensive preparations of documents in multiple languages for the minister of Telecommunications and the Prime Minister, another unplanned meeting occurred. Mother reported,

> Thursday, May 16 – That evening about 6:30 p.m., a knock came at our door, and we found that the King of Burundi was at Kibimba with car trouble. The Rawsons gave him a cup of coffee while Bob put gas in our car and prepared to take him to Usumbura. We were introduced to him, and then Bob and Perry took him by the black top road. Bob took along the last copy of the three Radio Presentations and talked with him about the project and gave him the copies.

God's plan was clearly behind this chance meeting. Later, during the next ham radio talk with Grandpa and my cousin back in Texas, Mother summarized how God was working to bring the project into being:

> Sunday, May 19 – We went to Mweya, and we had a very good schedule with Stan and Leon. They had been working very hard to get together Ampex 351 tape recorders, a Gateway console, and other equipment to ship in June. We were very encouraged by their faith and promised to send a prayer letter to help raise funds needed.

The evidence of a unity of faith in God's work was shared by people on both continents as they did not wait for government approval for the station before they began to send some equipment that would be needed. They would need time to record all the programs they would later use when the station was running.

CHAPTER FOURTEEN

RAIN, MANY HELPERS, AND A CAR

From March through August of that year, Mom and Dad were focused on all aspects of communication with African Christian leaders and missionaries who gracefully gave of their time and talents to help make the radio project a reality. There were so many presentations, letters, incorporation documents, permits, and meetings that took a whole team of people with wonderful skills and connections to make the process work. The job would also require repeated trips up and down the mountains to meet and transport people. Mother's journal will have to serve to provide some of these details since I was in school:

> Saturday, March 9 – We left for Mweya where an all-day meeting was held to form policy for the whole mission. Bob was asked to speak to the missionary group at 8 a.m. concerning the radio project. A business meeting followed in Kirundi.

> Thursday March 14 – The first Executive meeting of CABCO was held. The group was organized and plans were made to make a formal presentation of the radio project to the Ministers of Education, Telecommunications, and the Prime Minister. These individuals had been briefed by Sindamuka, and they seemed favorable if it meant progress in Burundi.

Monday, March 18 – We spent most of the morning studying Kirundi while Bob wrote the presentation for the radio project. I typed it or half of it, and that afternoon Randall Brown and Michelle Gruez began translation into French. Janine Gruez typed it.

Wednesday, March 20 – We left early for Usumbura and went down on the black-top road. The road was slick and bad in spots, but we came down without delay.

Saturday, March 23 – We stopped to see Sindamuka and received a report that he and Stanley had studied the presentation and had felt that they must not be proud, but they must kneel down and thank God for the possibility of radio in Burundi and asked that God bring it to pass. A rain storm came up, so we decided to stay at Vugizo for the night.

Wednesday, March 27 – We went to Usumbura with the Browns. We made investigation for getting a car.

Thursday, March 28 – We did business in Usumbura, applied for a new Volvo at the dealers. That night we went over the presentation, and Stanley made vital suggestions for improvement.

Friday, March 29 – The presentation was retyped and given to Sindamuka. We spent the day getting business done including a Power of Attorney. When we started up the mountains, a huge rainstorm turned us back for the night. We ate supper at a hotel and went to bed at Vugizo. The staff held a special prayer meeting at Kibimba. The Thornburgs and Ralph Choate were there, and there was a special meeting.

Tues, April 2 – The Alliance Meetings were in session at Usumbura, so we saw many other missionaries and talked with them concerning the radio project. Sindamuka reported that he had made a preliminary report or presentation to the Minister of Telecommunications. We went to see a 1962 Opal that had been bought by Justin Pierre last December. We made arrangements to buy it the following morning.

Wednesday, April 3 – We spent the morning transferring the car – we had found almost an impossible car. The Belgian had kept it in top shape and made some fine improvements. We took our shipment lists to AMI and learned that our shipment should be in Dar Es Salaam the next day. We spent the rest of the day getting flour, groceries, and needed supplies. That night Sindamuka reported a very favorable reaction from the Minister of Telecommunications. We thank the Lord!

Friday, April 5 – We returned to Kibimba that afternoon with Bahenda in our new car.

Thursday, April 11 – We went to Usumbura at noon. We had a CABCO Executive Meeting in the evening. We discussed the proposed law and decided to seek an appointment with the Prime Minister the following Wednesday morning.

Friday, April 12 – We picked up Bahenda to return to Kibimba. The rain prevented this, so we rested, did business, and left again in the evening.

Saturday, April 13 – We left for Kibimba at 2:00 p.m. After about an hour drive we came to a landslide area which is called the Mud Hole. Paul Thornburg got stuck, so we waited about an hour before we got through fine with chains on.

Tuesday, April 23 – We went at noon to Usumbura where we looked at property available for Cordac Institute and a medium wave station location. We saw a property which looked like a very suitable place for our proposed activities: three apartments, offices, showroom, shop, and warehouse. We will pray about this and trust the Lord will supply our needs.

Wednesday, April 24 – Bob confirmed with Stanley concerning details about the radio school.

Thursday, April 25 – The Prime Minister received Bob and Randall and made the request that a detailed presentation be compiled to help the Ministers in knowing what our proposed plans consisted of.

Monday, April 29 – The coming days were spent in writing and rewriting the details of Cordac Institute and details on the suggested schedule for building a radio station here. David Riley helped by translating it into French. Janine Gruez typed it in French, and I typed it many times in English until it reached its final form.

Thursday, June 6 – The Cordac meeting in the evening revealed that there was talk of drastic changes in the Burundi government, and we were not sure where this left Cordac.

Friday, June 7 – We heard that the Prime Minister and his cabinet had resigned.

> Monday, June 10 – I began copies of the CORDAC Five Year Plan and the Radio School of Arts and Sciences. I did not know French.
>
> Thursday, August 29 – We prepared the Letter of Request for Authorization of radio stations and went to Hotel Paguidas for a meal and to sign the letters.
>
> Friday, August 30 – Bob and Nkundwa delivered the Letters of Request and Incorporation Letters for the radio station to the office of the King, Prime Minister, Ministers of Telecommunications, Justice, Education, and Interior.

At that time, a series of days held celebrations. My mom's birthday was September 1, and my parents' anniversary was on September 2. They didn't know they would have another reason to celebrate the next day too. Mom's diary describes the lovely cake and gifts for her birthday, the open house with homemade ice cream she made herself and cake baked and decorated by Mae Kellum. I was still at home for our break.

> Tuesday, Sept. 3 – Franchise granted! Letter of Authorization dated this date.

After the prayerful celebration, they took us kids to school and began a whole new set of letters and translations. They would be busier than ever. The property they had considered was approved for purchase, and the equipment had already started to come. Mom and Dad moved down to the property in Bujumbura and began working from there. Now they could avoid so much traveling up and down the mountains, but they had a radio station to build and a technical school to start. Their students would be getting hands-on training with the equipment as well as classroom lessons.

CHAPTER FIFTEEN

GIVING THANKS AND BUILDING A STATION

After the prayers of thanks to God, there were many people to thank and announcements to be made. The government wanted to know the timeline for beginning the radio station. More equipment would have to be ordered, and the property to house it would have to be finalized. Securing an antenna site and getting government permission was also required. There was much more work to be done. Here are some of the key details from my mother's diary:

> Wednesday, Sept. 4 – Cordac meeting – we decided to request the Board at home to buy the new property.
>
> Friday, Sept. 6 – We went to Mweya to mimeograph a letter to announce the receipt of the franchise. We had to make up letterheads, write the letter, and have it translated into Kirundi, so we did not finish it until Saturday.
>
> Sunday, Sept. 8 – We had a prayer and praise service that afternoon at the Kibimba church. Friends came from Kibuye and Mweya, and the service was climaxed with an offering spontaneously from Africans and

missionaries. That evening we all ate together in the Kellum front yard. It was a wonderful time of fellowship.

Wednesday, Sept. 11 – Bob, Paul Thornburg, and Bahenda called on the Prime Minister to thank him for the authorization to build radio stations in Burundi. He asked when we might be on the air. We replied that he hoped to have a small transmitter on by Christmas and a larger one by Easter. He revealed the intense interest of the government in the project and the importance of getting on the air as soon as we could with as much power as we could.

Saturday, Sept. 14 – We went to Mweya to work on translation of the Cordac Executive Meeting Minutes. Bob wrote the thank you letter to the Prime Minister, and Leroy Little helped to translate it into French.

Saturday, Sept. 21 – We had a ham schedule with the folks in Texas. And they gave us the good news that a unanimous decision had been made to purchase the new property – a real step of faith.

Monday, Sept. 23 – We went with Paul Thornburg and Bahenda to Usumbura to finalize the purchase of the new property. This was finally done by late afternoon when we moved into the upstairs apartment. We were visited by Stanley R. and his wife that evening, and we went to the Hotel Strabros for supper. While there, we saw the Prime Minister and three or four key governmental people (Head of Parliament, etc.).

The radio station was to be one of three Christian stations on the continent of Africa. Several others had attempted to get a franchise in Burundi, which had a large population of Christians, but they had not received approval until that time. Many Africans and missionaries had coordinated their efforts, and God had brought it into being. The recording studio was set up in the warehouse on the property, and antenna sites were approved by the minister of telecommunications. The technical school for training African men to learn all aspects of programming and technical support Mom and Dad would teach began in a room across the compound.

Radio Cordac staff

Mom and Dad at Cordac property, our apartment
upstairs and future Christian book store below

Taped messages and music are broadcast across the continent

An announcer presents the next program

CHAPTER SIXTEEN

NKUNDWA

As my parents began their work in Burundi, they had a great need for people with knowledge of the local languages. My mother began studying Kirundi right away, but it took some time to develop much ability to communicate effectively. One of the missionary ladies helped her learn at first, and Nkundwa taught her later as well. My father had admitted he had a weakness in learning a second language. Consequently, they sought out people who could interpret for them. My mother needed a teacher, and my father needed a translator when he preached, prepared documents, or had meetings with those who spoke Kirundi and French, but not English.

At first, different missionaries fluent in Kirundi would translate my father's sermons at different churches around the countryside. This arrangement worked for a while, but as more work was required to obtain government approval for the radio station, my father needed someone to work with him full time. The man who came to fill that need was Nkundwa, who was still going to the preaching school at Mweya. He was fluent in Kirundi, French, and English. Sometimes they would pick him up for the weekend, along with my brother and I, so he could help them translate some documents.

Once Nkundwa graduated, he began working full time and was given a place to stay with our family. There were native preachers and government officials my father could talk with in Kirundi or French through Nkundwa's interpretation skills. There were documents that had to be prepared, sometimes in Kirundi and sometimes in French. Working with my father, this man was a conduit for bringing verbal and written communications into existence. This was no small task for one man. Nkundwa became part of our family, traveling with us and making my parents' jobs possible.

Dad worked with Nkundwa, who translated from English to Kirundi, in preparing letters as Mom stated in her diary,

> Friday, August 29 – We prepared the Letter of Request for Authorization of radio stations and incorporation Letters to the office of the King, Prime Minister, Ministers of Telecommunications, Justice, Education, and Interior.

When the radio station opened, Nkundwa preached sermons on the air. Later Nkundwa was diagnosed with tuberculosis. He was confined to the room he stayed in, where my mother brought him his meals and medication. After several months, he was healed and returned to work.

When we finished our term in Burundi, Nkundwa stayed to continue helping with the radio station. He was a Hutu who married a Tutsi woman, and they had three children. Through the support of churches in the United States, his family, years later, moved to Texas, where he went to college for additional education. He returned to Burundi after two years of study, able to be an even greater help to the mission endeavors.

Nkundwa preaches live as Mom and Dad prepare music to follow

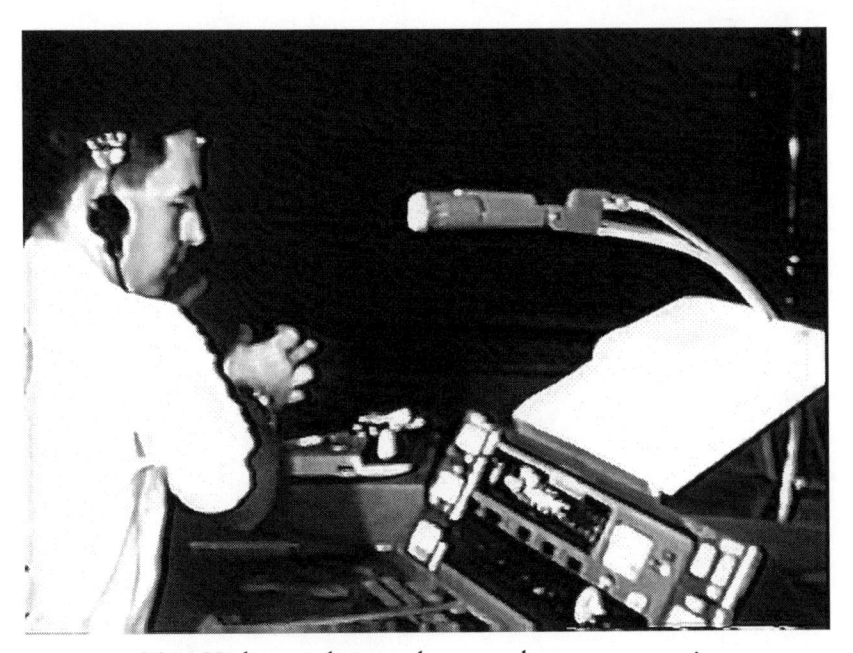

Tim Kirkpatrick introduces and prepares music

CHAPTER SEVENTEEN

MONKEYS AND BANANAS

Back in America, my favorite place to go in a zoo was the monkey cages. It is so surprising how well monkeys use their fingers to hold things in what I would have to call hands, not paws. They are so quick and agile holding on to branches and swinging up and down trees. Their faces also seem so humanlike, with a smile and a curious tilt of their head as they look at things or other creatures. Their ears are also shaped much more like human ears with a rounded top rather than a pointed one. They seem to have a sense of humor about what they do. At least they make me laugh.

There are many forms of monkeys in Africa, like chimpanzees, baboons, gorillas, and a host of others, but most of them in Burundi are the smaller varieties. The rural people would capture some of them and try to sell them to foreigners who cared to buy them. When I was at home in Bujumbura for our vacation, I would wander around looking for things to do. I walked around to the back side of our yard where I saw an adult gray monkey tied to a tree outside my bedroom. I would visit it, but it was not friendly, and I did not try to pet it. I wondered who put this guy there, but he was not cute with his mouth open wide and all his teeth showing while he screeched at me. My guess was he had been placed there to serve as a guard dog of sorts, since the tree was close to my upstairs bedroom window. Throwing him a banana was the only thing I could think to do before I walked away. I want to mention the small bananas grown here were the most flavorful ones I have ever tasted. They have a tangy sweetness no other type of bananas could come close to. There are some small bananas in America, but they are not the same at all. I would give Africa the award for the best bananas in the world.

Anyway, one morning I saw a man with a baby monkey on his shoulder came into the compound with the other vegetable salesmen, so I ran up to him to see if this monkey was nice or mean. It seemed tame and unafraid of people. It had tiny black hands and feet. An unusual characteristic I noticed was beneath the mottled gray hair was bright blue skin. Really! It seemed to smile at me with its black mouth. I somehow talked my parents into letting me have it, which began a close relationship. It cuddled into my lower left arm as if my arm was a tree branch or the back of his mother. As its head snuggled into the crook of my arm and its eyes looked up at me, my mothering instincts kicked in quickly. We were inseparable throughout the day.

I walked around the building and over to my mother's office to visit her and show him off. The radio station had started broadcasting, and Mom was now the programming director and a teacher for the radio training school. There was a crowd of African men and women dressed in modern clothing surrounding my mother's desk. My mother's job was to organize each session in the recording studio and file the tapes for the radio station. Africans came from around the area and from other nearby countries to take turns recording sermons or group songs. They would wait for her to tell them when it was their turn to enter the recording room. There was a recording console and windows to allow observation of those being recorded and to view the cue signals from the man at the console. The equipment was operated by African men or sometimes by the other missionary, Tim Kirkpatrick, who worked with us at the radio station. The people who came to record may have been using Swahili, Kiswahili, or Kirundi. Occasionally, hymns in English or French on records would be used, but mostly the programs were in the native languages. This station had a short-wave signal, which meant it traveled farther to other countries. A second tower provided a long-wave signal for the immediate area. There were also medium-wave signals to blanket all Central Africa. Native people from churches in these counties would be invited to come and record live sermons or music in our studio. Many had traveled from far away to be able to supply programs. As I left my mom's office area, I would wave and smile at the crowd of people, say something to my mom, and go back to the house to play with my monkey and my two brothers.

Usually playing on the floor with little metal cars, my brothers barely noticed me. I would sit on the floor and watch them, usually feeling sleepy from the heat. Bujumbura was much hotter than at our school because the altitude was much lower, and the heat was penetrating. We were privileged to live in a wonderful fully furnished European-styled house, minus any fans or air conditioners. We were grateful for the nice breezes that came through the windows, but the upstairs was cooler than my brothers' room downstairs. I felt my feet swelling in the heat and was glad I didn't have to keep my shoes on.

Before I fell asleep, I went to my dad's office, which was next to my brothers' room. When I took my monkey in to see him, he was busy writing something as usual. He was often preparing flyers to send to my grandpa in Texas, where they would be printed on a full-sized printing machine like the ones used to print newspapers. There was such a printing machine filling up an entire room on the ground floor of my grandparents' house back in Texas. Grandpa Perry did all the printing work himself and mailed the flyers to churches and individuals that supported the radio station. This was the lifeline to financial support for the radio project and the missionaries' salaries. Dad was the director of the whole station in Burundi as well as coordinating all communication to gain support from America. Our family was in this country to transmit the Gospel to those who had not yet heard it or to those who had become Christians and needed encouragement. The people here were very receptive to Christianity, and there were many churches growing and developing, but there were areas where people had no access to a Bible or a church. I passed by Dad and waved as I walked through. He seemed very happy to be serving people in such a way.

I took my monkey upstairs to my room and rested in the cooler air as a breeze blew through the window. Our house was an apartment above a former business space. There were additional rooms on the first floor behind the business area where my brothers had their room and my father had his office. The property purchased for the radio station had been abandoned the previous year by a Belgian camera salesman when Belgium gave Burundi its independence. He had served the tourists who came to this country to go on safaris in nearby animal preserves and national parks. The Belgian man even left behind a movie camera, which delighted my father, since he was a camera buff, and a film could serve as a fine way to inform churches in America of what was being done in Burundi to present the Gospel. Making a movie that presented the radio project was clearly on his to-do list. He did complete that film later, which was shown to supporters in America. For the previous owner, the largest city and economic hub of Burundi, Bujumbura was a convenient place for tourists to fly into Central Africa to begin sightseeing in the most famous national animal reserves to the east. Conveniently, the three buildings used before to store equipment were connected by a security wall, providing a safe area in the city for us to live and work. There was a second apartment for the Kirkpatricks, the other missionary couple, and a room below them for a classroom used to train some of the Burundian men who worked with us. Part of the agreement with the government when they approved the radio station was to provide a school to teach their own people how to run the station themselves. The students also worked for Cordac as they studied. My parents were glad to do that. Later other missionaries involved added a Christian bookstore in the front business area below our apartment. It also provided a reading area and correspondence course lessons. The property was just the perfect type of place that served the many needs of the radio station and staff. There was no doubt this property was God's blessing.

One morning before my month-long vacation ended, I woke up and went outside to get my baby monkey, but I could not find him. I never saw him again, but I suspected someone took him to be sold to another little girl whose family lived in the city, or he escaped to the tall trees, especially the banana trees.

My blue-skinned monkey with a tasty banana

Dad presents the plans for the radio station to Bahenda, a preacher and member of the Cordac Executive Board

Children singing in recording studio

Bob, Neil, Marilyn, Paul, Esther Kellum

CHAPTER EIGHTEEN

GOING ON SAFARI

Once I finished eighth grade at Mweya, I had to transfer to a new boarding school in Kenya. To take me there, our family had the most exciting vacation while we took a journey together through the Serengeti of Tanzania, formerly known as Tanganyika. We would camp along the way and experience things Europeans long ago had planned for as a once-in-a-lifetime adventure. This was a no-frills version of the safaris enjoyed by wealthy tourists from around the world. They typically wore the khaki clothes and iconic safari helmet of similar color. Our family cared nothing for the fashion of those times as we ventured across the prairies; however, we were excited to see all the different animals on this vast and famous open lands that held almost any African animal one can think of.

Our travels would begin in Bujumbura, traveling east and slightly south across Burundi, into Tanzania and south of Lake Victoria, before we turned north to reach Nairobi, the capital of Kenya, and found our way to my new school. The five of us piled into our light blue VW van. We called it a Combi. Mom and Dad were in front, while my two brothers and I sat on the one hard bench seat. All the windows were open to let in any breeze. Tanzania consisted of flat open plains with tall dry grass and a very few flat-topped trees that looked like they were suffering for water. It was August, so the dry season was about to end. There were no hills to be seen anywhere across the horizon. While Burundi was lush with green vegetation and mostly covered with mountains, Tanzania was mostly light brown, all flat, few villages, and devoid of towns or farms through this vast open region. If we had problems along the way, we were on our own. Our excitement for the adventure we were about to experience was not dampened by this situation. This part of the world seemed so big and free, like no place we had ever been before.

As we drove our Combi on the dirt roads, we saw hundreds of Thomson's gazelles grazing together. This species of gazelle is smaller than others and marked by one striking wide horizontal stripe of black. They have a tan back and white belly and legs. Their thin horns have a slight curve to the back. Lions and cheetahs would hunt them, but these gazelles had great speed and numbers.

Some male lions could be found napping under trees in the shade, while the females prowled around together, looking for slower or younger animals that might be easy prey. When they made a kill, the male lions, along with the females and cubs, would move in to devour their share. If the whole pride was napping together, we knew they had eaten their dinner. Even then, we never got out of the vehicle. Spotted cheetahs, the fastest of the wild cats, could chase full-sized gazelles and catch them single-handedly. Hyenas would clean up the leftovers, followed by the vultures. I respected the lions and cheetahs for their athletic ability and majestic mannerisms, but I found the hyenas sinister and creepy.

Surprisingly, the hippopotamus is the most dangerous of the wild animals because of their huge size. They are only found in or near a river or lake. They seem like lazy fat beasts, but many fishermen have been killed by them because they are hard to see under the water. Their heads might be the only part of them showing, and they blend in with the water and rocks. Their mouths could chomp the bones and half a man's body in one bite. They do not eat meat; they eat vegetation found on land near the water in the middle of the night because they are very sensitive to the sunlight. They attack people because they are mad they are being bothered in their territory. They are hunted for their huge teeth and tusks that are ivory like the elephant's tusks. Also found only in or near the water are the crocodiles. They are more agile than the hippos, but the monstrous size of the hippos would outdo the crocs several times. The crocs did eat meat though.

Before our trip, we were told we should be careful not to drive close to the giraffes. They had been known to become agitated by vehicles enough to jump on the top of open jeeps to injure people and to even cause wrecks for closed vans or trucks. When we looked at the giraffes eating from the tops of trees, we began to appreciate the size of these beasts and believe these stories.

When we stopped at the side of the road for supper and a place to sleep, we gathered our food from the ice chest and started a fire before dark. Our camping spot was right out on the open prairie. We set up our tent for Dad and my brothers. I was glad Mom and I got to sleep in the van because we had all heard a story of a man being pulled by the head out of his tent by a lion. Consequently, we kept the fire going for good reason.

The next day we moved on to see more animals and enjoy the views. When we came to a thicket of trees, we came rather close to a lioness stalking a warthog. Dad turned off the engine so we could watch the chase without distracting either animal. All of us watched intently as the lioness came closer to its prey. It seemed inevitable the lioness would catch the smaller animal that would have no real defense, except its short tusks. Somehow the warthog dodged into a thicket just right, and the lioness slowed down to search for it. Eventually turning away, the lioness had given up this tasty morsel. We were kind of happy for the warthog until Dad tried to start the engine, and it would not turn over. He tried again as we looked around at one another and back at the lioness. Yes, we were going to have to get out and push. We slid the side door open and quietly but quickly ran to the back of the van. Pushing as hard as we could, we listened closely for the engine to start as we got closer to the lioness. We heard the welcome hum and jumped back into the van. Dad put it in gear, and off we went, feeling relieved the lioness had not become interested in us, even if we had been pushing straight toward it.

Elephants were more plentiful to the north of the Serengeti, in areas around Lake Victoria, which was mostly adjacent to Uganda. We didn't see elephants in the wild like we saw so many other species that traveled in large herds. They stayed farther north, especially during dry season. Wildebeests, wild buffalo, zebras, and different species of gazelles would cluster together and create a thunderous sound when they began to run. These animals could charge long distances at amazing speeds. They had their enemies, but lions would only consider catching the young or the feeble that became separated from the others. Their biggest challenge for them was probably finding enough grass to feed so many, especially in the dry season. Perhaps their greatest strength was in their numbers.

Monkeys were rare on the open plains with few trees. Naturally, they mostly preferred jungle areas, where trees and fruit were plentiful. We never saw chimpanzees or gorillas, which were more common in the thick jungles of the Congo. However, baboons roamed in small groups in the Serengeti. I found them entertaining to watch as they walked across the grass with their hairless butts in the air as proud as can be. I laughed inside and felt a little embarrassed for them.

When we reached the Kenya border, we turned north to Nairobi, a capital city much larger than Bujumbura. The first thing we wanted was fresh meat, which we found in a casual restaurant somewhat like our American barbeque places. Here, we found actual grocery stores with ready-made snacks, like chips and candy bars we had not tasted since arriving in Africa. We picked out all we were allowed to get. The final day of my part of the trip was the next morning, when we drove about an hour to Rift Valley Academy, the only American-style school serving all the countries of Central Africa. When we arrived, I was shown to my dorm, and the rest of my family began their drive back to Burundi. I would be staying at this school for three months without weekend trips home, but what a trip we had together!

CHAPTER NINETEEN

RIFT VALLEY ACADEMY

My family hugged me and left me at the girls' dorm of Rift Valley Academy in Kenya. I had my clothes, my snacks, and a short-wave radio. I would have to wear the school uniform, which was a white cotton shirt with a red ribbon attached at the top button and a gray wool jumper with a school insignia patch on the left side. The school provided education for students from elementary through high school from countries across Central Africa. It served English-speaking students, mostly American missionary kids. We did have one African girl who had received an education like ours. She spoke with a British accent. There was another missionary girl who was my friend from Mweya in Burundi. We shared a bunk bed.

Since this school served students from several countries, there were full classes for each subject in each grade in high school. This school's goal was to provide a quality education that would prepare us to succeed in American schools whenever our parents returned to the United States. Some students graduated from high school and returned to the American college they had applied to and were accepted. We had several American teachers who had dedicated their career to prepare us well, whether we would return to a life in America or become missionaries in foreign countries around the world like our parents. While my sixth through eighth grade years had been rather untraditional or "old school," this school was more like schools back in the United States. I felt stimulated by the different teachers who were obviously gifted and knowledgeable of their subject. I remember our geometry teacher going over a process of solving a math problem, while I felt an awakening to the practical purpose of figuring out the answer to the problem. My favorite teacher was my English teacher, and while I enjoyed math, I made up my mind to become an English teacher, hopefully for a high school. On Sunday mornings, the teachers would open their houses for students to visit them for coffee before church. This situation provided me with my first taste of coffee, with a lot of sugar and cream, of course. I admired the dedication of our teachers to serve our educational needs and to develop a personal relationship with us. They were good role models for me in their hard work and personal interest in us as I prepared for a future in education. My father told me one time that education was a mission too.

The girls' dorm had the best location on campus, looking over the huge Rift Valley from atop a hillside. The full-length porch was a great place to stand and look out to see the inactive volcano and lake in the valley. It was a million-dollar view. Our porch had been designated as the place for couples to meet and talk in the evening. There was a boy I liked who had been at my school in Burundi. We had given each other some notes while we were there like we had done back at Mweya. We were very shy, although our families frequently had spent time together. I gave him a note one day at this school, asking him to meet me on the porch, but he did not answer. I guess we were not ready to share our feelings in a face-to-face conversation yet.

I did get a little homesick sometimes there, especially at night. Many times, my dorm mother at Mweya had come to say good night and tickle us or tuck us in before we went to sleep. Also, my parents would take us home for the weekend or visit us when they came to talk on the ham radio to family in Texas. At this school in Kenya, though, I would be staying a full three months before our break to go home. Listening to my short-wave radio became my nighttime routine. I would turn it on once I got in bed and tune in to Radio Cordac. The sign-off song played every night was the "Hallelujah Chorus," sung by a large choir in English. The word "hallelujah" is the same in every language. My homesickness was healed as I listened, and I felt a special joy in this song that praised God and expressed such admiration of Jesus. The words came from the Bible, describing the singing there would be in heaven.

The Heart of Africa

"King of kings, and Lord of lords," (Rev. 19:16b) "Hallelujah!" (Rev. 19:1b).

At the end of each three-month term, the three of us from Burundi would fly back together to Bujumbura from Nairobi. We were glad we had one another as we had a stopover in Entebbe Airport in Uganda, which was known for its dictatorial government. As we landed in Uganda's airport, we disembarked the plane guarded by soldiers with rifles. Three fifteen-year-old kids huddled together walking down the steps from the plane and found the desk where we would have to fill out papers declaring how much money we had as well as anything that might not be allowed. We sat down together to complete our papers and then turned them in before we looked for our next plane to take us to Burundi, where we would be met by armed guards again. We were all glad to see our families and enjoy our month at home.

While we were at home during our school break, we spent our time in a variety of activities. During my eighth and ninth grade years, I had committed to a personal goal to read the whole Bible and take notes each day. I read five chapters a day and wrote a paragraph summary. During this vacation time, I expanded my daily sessions to more chapters. Also, we would get together with other missionary kids and play board games. We even made our own game with a board and marker pieces. It was a little like Monopoly, only the board was a map of the world where we could buy a country instead of a street. Looking back, I am rather horrified we would create a game that demonstrated such a motive. Another game we played included a wooden game board with cups carved out and with little stones in the cups to move around the board as we played Mancala, a game that originated in Africa. Sometimes we would beg our parents to take us to the other missionary family's house in Bujumbura, but we were often told they had no time to take us, or they couldn't afford to pay for the gas, even if our friends lived only about a mile away. We were not allowed to walk outside the walls of the compound by ourselves. So, we found something to do together at home. Soon our break would be over, and I would return to our school in Kenya, while my brothers would return to the school in Mweya.

CHAPTER TWENTY

A HIKE IN RIFT VALLEY

One special Saturday, some of the students, including myself, were bussed down from our school at the top edge of Rift Valley, which faced a volcano across the valley. The girls were privileged to live in a dorm that had a huge back porch facing this breathtaking panoramic view. On one side of the inactive volcano was a small lake covered with pink flamingos. Can you imagine a lake virtually covered with pink birds so far away that we could only see the pink color covering the water? Our bus would take us into the valley to the base of the volcano, where we would begin our hike up the side.

We gathered at the base of the volcano and looked up to judge the steepness of the climb. It was more like hiking up a high grassy hill, not like climbing a rocky mountain. We were not athletes, but we were young and tough. As we began the climb, it was just a matter of putting one foot in front of the other with our bodies slanted forward for balance. We would pause from time to time to catch our breath and rest a little, but we kept a steady pace until we reached the rim of the volcano.

Reaching the rim, I began to feel overwhelmed by my fear of heights. There was a nice flat path all the way around the rim, but the sheer straight drop to the bottom of the caldera made me wonder if I could go on. The path was barely a foot wide, so I gathered up my nerves and tried to keep my eyes on the path rather than looking down the frightening sheer rock slope. I worked hard to keep my balance while

I put one step in front of the other. When I did stop to look down, I could see the bottom of the crater was covered with tall lush green trees. The richness of the ground fertilized by lava made the bottom a wonderful place for vegetation. I began to wonder if falling on the tops of these trees would cushion me much, and I decided the trees would not help me survive.

Consequently, I kept walking carefully and trying not to go so slow that the kids behind me would think I was scared. I probably held my arms out like a tightrope walker when I felt myself leaning. If I stopped to look out over the valley, I would step away from the steep edge to feel more balanced before I raised my eyes and looked around. The hike around the rim seemed much longer and more physically challenging than climbing to the rim because we were straining to keep our balance, even though we did not have a steep climb, except one area where there was a peak. I had managed to walk all the way around the rim, only to realize hiking downhill took a balancing act too but without the psychological challenge of acrophobia.

Our group was hot and tired when we got back to the bus. We felt proud we had completed our hike without any accidents. I would always remember our successful hike up and around the volcano and would think of this day every time I looked out across this beautiful valley.

Rift Valley volcano rim

Our hiking group prepares to climb the peak.

CHAPTER TWENTY-ONE

OTHER PLANS

We had been in Burundi for four years. Like other missionaries, we were scheduled to return to the United States for what missionaries called furlough. Radio Cordac had been on the air for almost three and a half years. Other missionaries and trained Africans would continue the work. Our family would return to Texas, where we had lived before, and I would continue my high school education there.

After packing our suitcases, we went to bed to rest before our long flight. Like other trips, we took advantage of our trip to schedule tours of important places that might be convenient stops along the way. Our first stop was to be Cairo, Egypt, where we planned a tour of the pyramids and other ancient structures along the Nile. Our second stop was going to be Israel, where we could see the places where Jesus lived and taught. Along with seeing Jerusalem, we would see Bethlehem, Old Jericho, and other areas before we returned to Jerusalem to have a taxi drop us off at the border crossing into Jordan. No car was allowed to drive across the border, so we would get out and walk to the other side. Finally, we would fly to Greece, where we could see Athens and some of the places where the apostles traveled to spread the Gospel. My father had savings from his inheritance years ago to be able to take this trip of a lifetime.

On the morning of our flight from Bujumbura to Egypt, we finished our packing and waited for our time to leave. Quite a crowd of people were planning to meet us at the airport to say goodbye. When we got to the airport, we talked to so many people and gave many hugs before we went to check in at the desk. Mom had the passports and other paperwork in her purse. She pulled out each item for the five of us as she was asked for them. "Tickets … Tickets …" Mom looked through her paperwork and dug back into her purse—no tickets.

Thus began a very disappointing and embarrassing moment. We were missing our tickets, and we lacked the time to go back to get them. Mom and Dad looked at each other and had to explain we were going to have to change our flight to Egypt to the next day. We got our flight cancelled and changed as needed. In a very anticlimactic moment, we gathered up our suitcases again and were driven back to our house. The road from the airport was as straight and flat as the landing strip it paralleled. Equally monotonous was the lack of trees or green things of any kind. Only an uncomfortable silence surrounded us in the car. When we got back home, Mom went straight to the top drawer of their dresser to find the missing tickets. There they were as she expected. We felt like strangers in our own house as we went back to our old rooms with our suitcases and awkwardly went to bed for a rather restless night.

As I was trying to get to sleep, knowing we would have a long day since we would have a layover at the airport in Cairo without the exciting tour, I focused on the night's silence. Suddenly, I heard a rattle at the patio door that opened to the living room. A couple of minutes later, I heard a loud crack in the hallway between my bedroom and my parents' bedroom. Then I heard more scuffling and voices on the porch. My dad had heard the noise as well and had come out of his room to check it out. A loud clapping sound split the night air and scared me. Confused, I cracked open my door and peeked out gingerly. On the floor in front of my dad was a long bamboo fishing pole we had planned to leave behind. It had been leaning upright against the hallway wall where Dad had knocked it over while he was checking on things. Our attention was shifted to the porch as two young African men had climbed up a large tree close to the porch and attempted to get into the house. Dad and I saw them run back to the edge of the porch, and we heard the men as they jumped off the porch, skipping the tree route to get down the quickest way possible. As we deduced from their speed, they must have thought they had heard a gunshot and didn't think about how far down their jump would be.

Later, as we talked about this event, we supposed the people in the area knew we were leaving and thought they were entering an empty house. We felt God had protected us every day while we lived in this country and knew He had taken care of us one more night.

The next day we gathered up our belongings once again and loaded our suitcases in the friends' car to go to the airport once again. There were a few less people this time, but we understood it would be hard to take two days off to say goodbye. This time we had our tickets, passports, and papers declaring any significant property in our possession. We hugged everyone again and knew that we would really be leaving this time. Strangely, we felt relieved we were prepared this time but sad to end this special experience in our lives in this special country with a very special people, many of whom loved the Lord.

With less fanfare, this time we boarded the plane and said goodbye to our treasured homeland. I was so glad for the learning experiences and the strength of character Burundi had offered me. Besides having dedicated teachers in school, I felt even the fearful moments had brought me to a place in my teenage years where I would look to God for my needs and trust Him to take care of us.

Landing at Cairo's airport, we got off the plane to wait for a couple of hours. We looked through the windows and out across the desert sands to see if we could spot any of the pyramids, but they were too far away to see. We turned our thoughts to the most important visit we would make, the Holy Land. Our next flight took us to Israel, where we spent three days seeing significant sights mentioned in the Bible. In Jerusalem, we went to the top of what remains of Solomon's temple and looked around at the twelve gates of the city, which are central to many prophecies and events in the Old Testament. In a valley of the city, we saw the Garden of Gethsemane with two-thousand-year-old olive trees and the empty grave where Jesus was presumed to have been laid for three days before He arose, and we looked up at the nearby hill of Golgotha, which indeed looked like a skull, where Jesus was crucified. While inside the empty tomb, we were looking around in awe at the significance of this place when our contemplation was interrupted by what sounded like a cannon boom. Our minds tried to grasp what might be happening, imagining the second coming, but the tour guide explained to us the explosion sound was the signal of the end of the Muslim Ramadhan day, when they could break their fast for the day. We were rattled and confused by the loud noise in such a quiet, solemn place.

Traveling outside of Jerusalem the next day, we saw where Jericho had been before the Hebrews marched around and the walls fell and still lay in a pile that surrounds the remains of the abandoned city as God gave Joshua and Caleb victory over the Promised Land. The rubble pile lay undisturbed as a reminder of the power of God, and a new city of Jericho was built nearby. This unusual Bible story might be more amazing, knowing the old city had two walls, from two to six feet thick, with houses in between them and inside both. It was built to be completely impregnable unless someone let them in with a rope. Later we saw Bethlehem, where a small cave was believed to have held the animals and the manger where Jesus was laid at His birth. Unlike the simple barns that are usually part of the manger scenes displayed in many homes, we learned animals were usually kept in an underground area below the houses. There is also a beautiful church built in this town as a tribute to Christ's birth. I felt the impact of the Bible's stories and lessons as we saw these places we had read about. We stayed in an inexpensive hostelry rather than a hotel for the days we were in Israel. When we were driven to the border, we walked across to Jordan's checkpoint, since no one was allowed to drive back between the two countries. I had to agree with my father that, for a Christian, to see the lands of the Bible was the trip I would treasure always in my memory. I know this was the trip my dad had waited for and dreamed of for years.

Our trip to Greece was also a concrete history lesson of some of the places the apostles traveled to as they took the gospel to the Gentiles. We saw Athens and Corinth, where the apostle Paul preached to the Greeks who worshipped idols. Both cities were filled with statues and temples of the Greek gods. I remember my little brother, Paul, getting lost at the Acropolis. We later teased him about this incident after our fears subsided when we found him. As our momentous visits to key biblical places ended, we flew on to London, New York City, and Houston. Like our flights to Africa, we faced a shocking weather change from the heat of Africa to colder temperatures of Israel and even colder temps in New York. At last, we were in Texas and back with Grandpa and Grandma.

CHAPTER TWENTY-TWO

AS THE YEARS GO BY

Our family never returned to Burundi, although my father worked full time for about two years to support the work overseas. He opened and operated two Christian bookstores and later a business selling pop-up campers made by a Christian company. He continued to support various churches and organize weekend conferences.

I became an English teacher, as I had planned since the sixth grade, and retired after forty years of teaching mostly senior English and advanced placement literature and composition, along with coaching academic competitors and directing theater arts for twelve Years. After retirement, I taught part-time at a community college. Tom, my husband, taught choir and computer literacy before becoming the director of technology for the school district. He retired from the same school district. My husband also served as song leader and youth director for our church youth groups until our two children were older. We took mission trips to remote areas in other states to host Bible schools in the summers.

My brother Neil worked with the camper business with my parents for a few years before moving on to a career in a copier corporation. He and his wife have been servants in their church through the years, and now, as they have retired, they have been supervisors and workers for team projects in Samaritan's Purse.

My other brother Paul chose to find a career in finance in Israel, where he worked in an electronics company and moved to a company called Mega Voice, which makes and distributes an audio device that reads the Bible in a chosen language to those who cannot read for themselves or do not have a Bible. These devices are particularly helpful to people who cannot read for themselves in underdeveloped countries or where missionaries are no longer allowed. He visited Burundi several years after we were there. My father was blessed to move to Israel to live with Paul's family for the last few months of his life. Paul worships with a church that consists mostly of Christian Jews and Arabs.

David and Mae Kellum were allowed back into Burundi in the early '80s, when no other protestant missionaries from America or Europe were there. They told us the Burundian Christian people treated them like family. They were invited to dinner and wedding ceremonies of the people there. Their three children went to Rift Valley Academy as I had. Some of the family members and other volunteers have returned to assist in the hospital run by a Burundian doctor in Kibimba. The country grants thirty-day visas to foreigners.

The Bible school for preachers is still in operation at Mweya, run by seasoned African preachers, but the missionary boarding school is closed.

Radio Cordac continued to broadcast Christian programs until 1977, when the government decided not to allow any radio stations not government controlled to operate. At that time, all foreign missionaries were forced to leave as well. Government leadership continued to change as the country shifted from an independent kingdom to a so-called democratic republic manipulated by outside countries in Europe and Asia. Various coups brought changes as the Hutu and Tutsi tribes continued uprisings, escalating to full civil wars to determine who was to take power rather than trusting in peaceful elections. In 1985, the prime minister was shot but not killed, initiating more violence in the country. After elections, the key political and military positions were announced to be won by the Tutsi, the favored minority tribe, which fueled the conflict between the two ethnic groups as it was clear to the Hutu tribe the results of the elections had to be false. While we were there in the '60s, we grieved as we heard reports or witnessed many Hutus, especially homes of trained Christian preachers, who were

The Heart of Africa

taken from their homes at night by militia, and they either starved in prisons or were shot there because they were deemed a threat to those in power. Preachers were a threat to the government because they were leaders of the people with more education to question the corruption. The Tutsis used their power to maintain control over the poor and less-educated Hutus. While we lived in Burundi, we knew of some African Christians who became victims of the ongoing strife. Reports of Burundian preachers disappearing in the night saddened our hearts for the loss of great men to their families and to the local churches. A soccer stadium in Bujumbura was known to have been struck by lightning, some said because it had been used as a place of execution. Thousands of Hutus had been imprisoned or murdered without any news reports through several years. As outsiders, we were always careful not to become involved in political matters or to report anything in letters or by other means. The government was known to open letters and punish anyone who sent out information about government activity.

While the Hutus had the overwhelming majority, the Tutsis always had the presidency until 1994, when the Burundian Hutu and the Rwandan Hutu presidents, the first Hutus to be declared winners of their elections, were flying home together from a peace conference in Kenya. A missile launched from the ground hit their plane, killing all aboard. Those responsible were never identified. The genocide of Tutsis by the Hutu militia took place in Rwanda after the double assassination was widely publicized in the news, even depicted in movies, around the world, but I must wonder why no reports of the hundreds of thousands of Hutus' deaths in Rwanda and Burundi over several decades were ever reported. In retrospect, I saw evil forces seek to turn the two ethnic groups against each other, believing they had been treated unfairly.

I know the poor unarmed Hutu farmers of Burundi did not participate in the violence. I must admit, while we were there, we never walked down the city streets alone, and we never drove anywhere at night as a precaution against dangerous encounters, but crimes among the common people were rare. The poor would always welcome visitors or neighbors in need into their huts to share what little they had. As missionaries, we were careful not to take sides or to discuss political issues, but we were aware of changes that meant more freedom and safety or less of each as the tide turned in leadership. We always respected and followed the laws of the country, carrying papers whenever we traveled.

Many years later some countries have tried to help develop roads, industry, and education, but others have taken advantage of the people and taken valuable resources in the guise of friendly assistance. As more countries around the world have laws against long-term missionaries, broadcasting Christian radio and delivering of Bibles or audio devices may be critical ways to help keep the church alive. Internet sources are available in the cities, but few have cell phones or computers. Rural areas still lack electricity, but most families have a battery-powered radio.

Nevertheless, native Christians continue to hold their faith in Jesus and worship in churches led by Burundian preachers. Some hospitals are run by native Christian doctors supported by churches abroad and assisted by volunteers from other countries who can stay on a thirty-day visa. More recently, David and Mae, along with other family and friends who were willing to go and serve as a team, have gone to help in the hospital in Kibimba. Through the support of their church in Chandler, Oklahoma, David and Mae assisted other volunteers who wished to help. Their son, Kelly, goes to Jordan and Kenya, where he serves some churches and organizes delivery of useful supplies. David's sister, Lorna, has returned to help at the hospital.

The college where my parents trained for service in Christian radio stations, called Azusa Pacific College, is still in operation. Christians who might consider mission work might realize from my story how missionary kids can have a blessed life and a unique education in seeing other places and cultures. There are far fewer countries now that allow full-time missionaries, but there are places that need help of all kinds. There are operating Christian radio stations around the world, including Far East Broadcasting Company, that send signals to closed countries.

While life in Burundi continues to be fraught with poverty and political unrest, the country has beautiful scenery and a flamboyant culture some tourists venture to enjoy. Still today, there are so few jobs or industries in existence that income is dismal for most natives. Since my brother Paul's visit to the country, he reported there is now more than one Christian radio station, and there are other radio stations as well. I wonder if some of the students my parents taught in the radio training school might be working in any of those stations. On the other hand, Burundian children still receive minimal education. Some of the young people can pay or receive donations to attend secondary school, where they might learn a trade or advance to a university, but most of them only complete six years of school and return to farming. Many families even strain to find the school uniforms required to attend primary school now, wearing oversized ones handed down from older siblings or friends.

As I think of those four years in Burundi, I know I was blessed with a world of experiences that taught me more than I might have learned anywhere else. Meanwhile, I feel a sadness that I enjoyed unique experiences few outsiders from abroad may ever be able to have in Burundi. Even more sharply, I feel concern for the people who may live on the brink of starvation, along with joy that Burundian Christians continue to keep their faith and pass it on. Clearly, I saw a people who had an enthusiasm for worship and a love for God that made them hope for peace more than any wealth or power. "Amahoro, Burundi." I wish you peace.

My heart will always hold a special place for the time I spent in the country of Burundi, whose people mostly remain untainted by the struggles and greed of the industrialized world yet whose simplicity holds them in poverty and inability to rise above the ethnic strife that has always afflicted them. I pray the Bible will continue to be taught in that land and that more souls will be faithful to the Gospel.

Faithful missionaries took the Gospel to the needy of Burundi. They took the message the Messiah had come to earth to save us from our sins by dying on the cross and rising from the grave to reign in heaven. They shared God's word that "Therefore if any man is in Christ, he is a new creature; the old things passed away; behold, new things have come. Now all these things are from God, who reconciled us to Himself through Christ, and gave us the ministry of reconciliation, namely that God was in Christ reconciling the world He has committed to us the word of reconciliation. Therefore, we are ambassadors for Christ, as though Christ, be reconciled to God. He made Him who knew no sin to be sin on our behalf, that we might become the righteousness of God in Him" (2 Cor. 5:17–21). This is God's eternal promise if we remain His faithful servants. I pray Burundi's people will continue to accept that promise, continuing the work of the church through God's grace. Pray for the peace of Burundi and that Christians in that land will share the truth of God's word and remain strong through all adversity.

Christians here in America today should seek out ways to support and encourage their fellow Christians in other lands. Please pray for the safety of African Christians, who have taken leadership to keep the churches alive in these needy lands. As Christians were told, "Do not neglect doing good and sharing; for with such sacrifices God is pleased" (Heb. 13:16). Burundi, as well as all countries, need the chance to hear the Gospel in some way. If your heart is touched to find a way to participate in a mission or in volunteering for medical work or donating to medical services, food provisions, or churches, I urge you to find a place to fill a need and rejoice in the part you play in serving God.

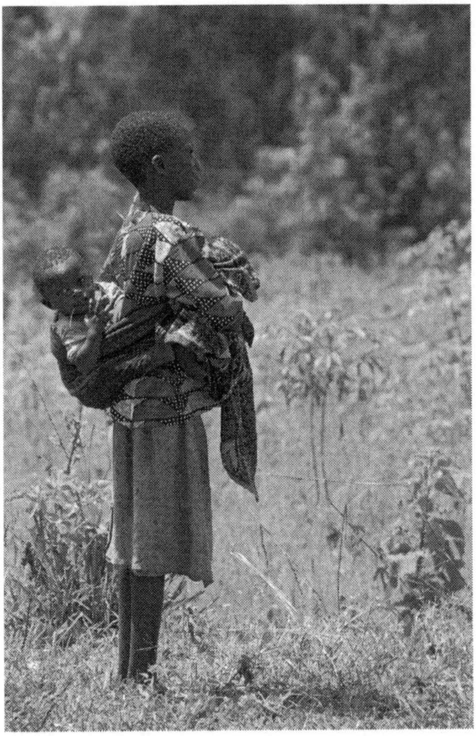

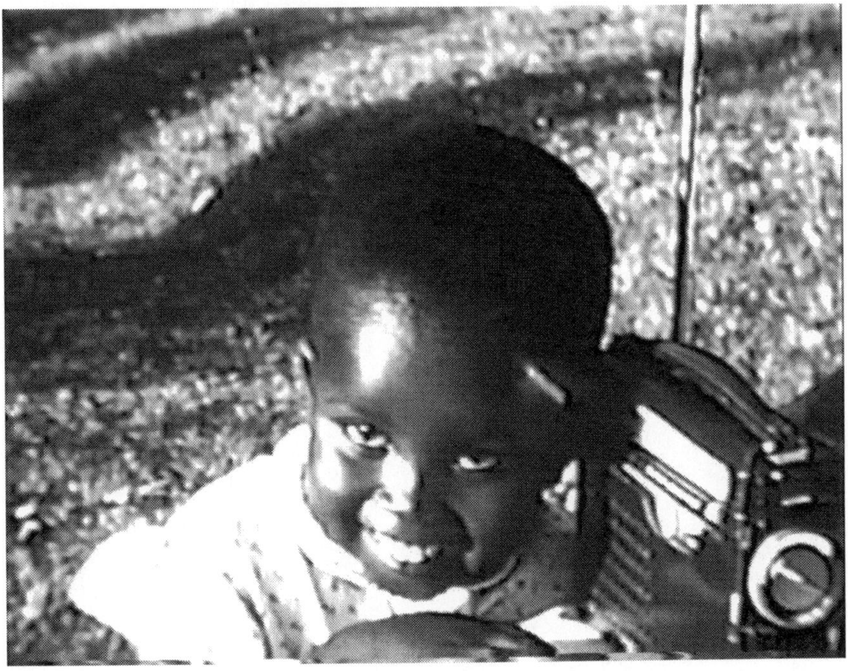

SUGGESTED PLACES TO CONTRIBUTE

Hospital in Kibimba, Burundi   (for service or donation, specify your purpose in communications)

Friends of Kibimba, 215 N. Blaine Ave., Chandler, OK 74834

Samaritan's Purse   (for service or donation to specific needs)
International Relief
samaritanspurse.org

Mega Voice International   (for donation of audio-Bibles in Kirundi and either French or English as a second language. Devices are also available for purchase in any two languages.)

Charles Cibene, Mega Voice International – cell# +1-954-937-8188

ccibene@megavoice.com

For check or wire transfer – Mega Voice International, 731 Duval Station Road, Suite 107-310, Jacksonville, FL, 32218

Pay Pal – log-on <http://megavoiceinternational.org/. click donate

Bank Account – Truist Bank, 3353 Peachtree Road, NE, Atlanta, GA 30326 USA

Swift Code SNTRUS3A

Routing 061000104

Account 246394232

SOURCES

Kellum, Esther Perry, *Diary*:1963.

New American Standard Bible, Foundation Press Publications, The Lockman Foundation: La Harra, California, 1971.

Made in the USA
Columbia, SC
02 July 2024